THE
SWEET APPLE
GARDENING BOOK

THE
SWEET APPLE
GARDENING BOOK

by Celestine Sibley

Illustrations by John Kollock

PEACHTREE PUBLISHERS, LTD.

Atlanta • Memphis

Published by
Peachtree Publishers, LTD.
494 Armour Circle, NE
Atlanta, GA 30324

Copyright © 1972, 1989 by Celestine Sibley
Epilogue © 1989 by Celestine Sibley
Illustrations © 1972, 1989 by John Kollack

This book was first published in 1972 by Doubleday & Company, Inc.

Manufactured in the United States of America

10 9 8 7 6 5 4 3 2

Designed by Patricia Joe

Library of Congress Cataloging-in-Publication Data

Sibley, Celestine.
    The sweet apple gardening book / by Celestine Sibley :
illustrations by John Kollock.
      p.   cm.
    ISBN 0-934601-68-2 : $12.95
    1. Gardening — Georgia.   2. Country life — Georgia.   3. Sibley,
Celestine   I. Title.
SB455.S44   1989
635.9'09758 — dc19   89-3048
                                                                CIP

ISBN 0-934601-68-2

For John, Bird, Sibley and Ted
in order of their appearance

Chapter 1

"For all true gardeners are only beginners and confidence in the future lightens their way like Pentecostal tongues of fire."

— Agnes Rothery in *The Joyful Gardener*

IT'S LATE SUMMER in the foothills of North Georgia and the early morning sun is slanting in over the pinewoods and through the poplar and sweetgum thicket at the edge of Sweet Apple clearing, laying long fingers of light across my little garden patch. It touched the cheerful faces of that hulking intruder, a volunteer sunflower, first, moving down to the hollyhocks and then to the zinnias and marigolds and now, as if a switch had been thrown by an adroit stagehand, it backlights the whole, edging in brightness the dark green of the mint bed, the gray green of chives and garlic, the crazy-quilt cushion of yellow nasturtiums, red petunias and blue ageratum.

From the screened porch where I sit snapping beans from a neighbor's garden I look at the light on my small garden, the rough grass, the crooked old peach tree leaning across the path and my heart lifts inside me in a great rush of happiness.

For the moment I am blessed among women—a gardener, a rich and successful gardener.

A mockingbird swaying high on the old apple tree melodically assures me it is so. The July flies, properly called cicadas, thrumming their tune of summer's ending in the woods, confirm it.

The fact that the beans I'm snapping came from a neighbor's garden casts not the slightest ripple on the deep pool of my content. My own beans just came in earlier, that's all, and not so profligately. Some gardeners grow beans, some button zinnias. Some grow spectacular watermelons, some exult over a volunteer vine that sprang up where the old compost pile was and has now climbed hand-over-hand to the top of a very tall pine tree, hanging swags of white bloom and tiny green pendant gourds all the way up.

It's not what you grow that makes you a rich and successful gardener, unless, of course, you are a pro, doing it for your livelihood. Some of my neighbors at Sweet Apple, farm-reared and still sustained all winter by what they produce in summer, regard my efforts as transient and grasshoppery.

To them that basket of tomatoes my six plants yielded up is not impressive—clearly not enough to can whole or convert to soup mix, juice or ketchup. But to me those tomatoes not only look like the crown jewels straight out of the Tower of London, blazing rubies of flawless texture and matchless symmetry, they will provide great dripping tomato sandwiches for lunch and a

bountiful salad for the twenty people who are coming to supper. And there are more where those came from, burgeoning green or slowly reddening on the vines.

It's the same with the four little rows of okra I will visit when the sun has dried the dew. To my neighbors caught up in late summer's frenzy of canning, freezing, pickling and drying, what I will gather will amount to a mighty puny harvest. But to me it will be more than sufficient to the day and the needs thereof—pointed green pods which I will harvest spendthrift small to dip whole in melted butter and lemon juice, allowing six to a dozen for each guest. I am prone to gloat over that okra patch, blooming and bearing at full tilt as it does, but I no longer liken the pods to tapered jade fingering pieces. For she who fingers fresh okra without wearing gloves itches miserably for hours.

Oh, there are prettier and more productive gardens all around me, all right, but the measure of success in gardening, like the measure of success in some other endeavors, is not always in the harvest.

A North Georgia mountaineer once explained to me about fishing. He said it was "a rare and comely day" in the spring and he found a seat on a big rock on the bank of a stream beneath the bee-busy shade of a blooming tulip poplar tree. The sun was warm on his shoulders, the stream at his feet sang sweetly, bees hummed in the flowers overhead and the pole in his hand had that feel of balance and rightness that is promising and unwearying.

"Feller passed and called out, 'How's the fishing?'" he related. "'Fishing's fine!' I called back. He said, 'How many you caught?' I laughed and told him straight: 'Nary a one. But I ain't never enjoyed fishing more.'"

So it is with gardening. The doing is the thing. And if by some happy chance you should have a little success, ah, the satisfaction that is!

IT's INCONCEIVABLE TO ME that there should be people in the world who are not attracted to and fascinated by the great natural laboratory of earth, water, sun and seeds. It's as if there were children who didn't like Christmas. I'm sure such people exist somewhere, just as there are probably children who sleep late on Christmas Day, but they are alien and exotic creatures beyond my experience.

It has little, if anything, to do with the fact that I am a southerner and the South has been a predominantly agricultural area until the last few years when sidewalks and paved roads began to catch up with row crops.

My great-aunt Babe, one of the first gardeners I remember noticing, lived in a small town. It's true that she and her husband owned a farm on the outskirts of the town, to which she drove a horse and wagon to gather fresh vegetables several times a week. But the small, town-sized lot on a street corner is what I remember. It had not a handful of dirt that wasn't sternly and lovingly commissioned to grow something.

Water oak trees, put out as striplings, outlined the fence and shaded street and sidewalk. Azaleas screened the foundation of the porch and eventually reached up to meet the overhang of the roof. Rosemary and sweet basil, bachelor buttons and old maids, spice pinks and verbena spilled over the walk. They didn't have plumbing in that little town when I was a child and the privy presented to

Aunt Babe a real challenge in landscaping, although she wouldn't have called it that.

The idea was to hide what was euphemistically called "the garden house" and the approach to it from the street. So Aunt Babe built a corridor of loveliness to The Edifice — trellises and fences freighted with rambler roses, morning glories and the dainty little cypress vine with its lacy foliage and star-shaped red and white flowers. Honeysuckle cascading over the roof served the double purpose of camouflaging the sturdy utilitarian building and perfuming the air — a useful service in those days before aerosol air fresheners.

The path to the privy was a delight to a child. The gate leading from the yard to the garden area was weighted to swing shut by an iron pot suspended on a chain between the gate and a post set in the ground. Some people further weighted the cracked pots they used on gates by filling them with horseshoes and rusty railroad spikes and other scraps of metal. Aunt Babe put dirt in hers and planted petunias — not the bright, rich-toned hybrids we know today but an old-fashioned kind that looked as if they had been faded in the wash — pallid bluish white and wan bluish lavender. They came back year after year, growing paler all the time but blooming prodigiously and smelling heavenly, particularly after a rain.

Sage and peppers grew by the gate — a potpourri of hot reds and yellows and cool gray-green colors and fragrances, which would show up again at hog-killing time when Aunt Babe mixed and ground and seasoned her incomparable homemade sausage.

Strawberries outlined the walk to the outhouse, offering bouquets of white flowers and red fruit simultaneously. She had more room for them out on the farm but she could not trust Will, the hired man, to maintain constant and unflagging vigilance against the jaybirds. So she planted strawberries where she could personally protect them, rushing out many times a day to flap a dish towel or a broom in the faces of the feathered marauders.

All children knew that jaybirds tattled to the devil, going every Friday to take him fat pine splinters to keep his fire going and an inventory of all our sins. I wouldn't have crossed a jaybird for all the strawberries or figs in the world but Aunt Babe either didn't believe in the jaybird mystique or wasn't scared of the devil. She fought for her berries, feeding them the richest cow manure and mulching them with the dark moist "rakings and scrapings" from behind the washhouse. This was where leaves and chinaberries, weeds and sweepings from the yard were piled and the laundry tubs were emptied. I know now that it was a compost pile of sorts but Aunt Babe called it her fish-bait bed, drawing from it not only the rich black earth for her strawberries and pot plants but fat rosy earthworms she would take to the creek bank when she needed respite from her gardening.

My mother, Muv, reared by her aunt Babe, had the same high regard for tilling the soil, and no lessons in practicality set for her by her husband could persuade her that it wasn't wise and thrifty to have a garden.

She married a city type with the kind of country connections that weren't strictly agricultural. His family owned a naval stores operation. He knew about converting pine trees into lumber and pine resin into turpentine and he worked very hard in an office, leaving the running of the pecan and satsuma orange groves, the corn and hay fields and the big vegetable gardens to field hands supervised by a Negro farmer named Joe Walker. Whatever was harvested in the fields found its way to our table and it seemed highly impractical to my father to hire somebody to plow and plant a garden back of our house.

"When you live in the country," said Muv firmly, "it's a sin not to have a garden."

Being wary of sin of any kind and reluctant to argue in any case, my father gave in and sent somebody with a mule to plow and turn our little patch every spring. My mother, after many happy winter evenings spent poring over seed catalogues from H. G. Hastings in Atlanta and Chris Reuter in New Orleans, had "ordered off" and was ready to greet spring by personally planting the garden. She also hoed and watered and proudly harvested it all by herself, except for what little work she could get from me and occasionally our cook and dear friend, Coot.

They say a lot now in city schools about the curiosity of the young child about growing things and his excitement in planting a little dried bean seed and seeing it sprout. I know this is true because the children in our family have demonstrated it to me. But I confess that my own sense of wonder was somewhat retarded. I think it was because my mother had me working too hard hauling bricks from old tumbled-down chimneys in the quarters to build walks in our yard and trundling barrow loads of bottles and cans out of a sinkhole down at the edge of the yard where she visualized a lily pond.

I was mortified as a teen-ager because our living room was always full of boxes of dirt in the wintertime. The magic of starting seeds early in flats and deploying them on sawhorses around the living room where they would catch the most sun may have been explained to me but I was slow to be ignited by the idea, particularly if there was a boy coming to visit.

Like all teenagers I wished my mother would be like other people's mothers and I didn't know a single one who was all that gung-ho about touch-me-nots being up and doing ahead of anybody else's. But after they were up and bedded out and blooming—earlier and bigger and better than any I'd ever seen—I was enormously proud of them and even of my mother.

Christmas vacations are for the most part seasons of anticlimax when the new wears off toys, visiting relatives go home and ennui sets in. There are only a few post-Yule holidays of my youth that I remember particularly and they happen to have been the ones spent in the woods or visiting old house sites collecting dogwood trees, crape myrtles and mountain laurels and transplanting them to our yard. Now I know that we should have planted them in clumps but we alternated a pink crape myrtle with a white dogwood all the way around the fence, banked the glossy evergreen mountain laurel around the eaves' drip line in front of the house and screened off the wall of the garage with a row of sweet shrubs and swags of Carolina jessamine.

Wildlings were not what my mother would have chosen if she'd had a choice. She visited nurseries in Mobile and she knew that ligustrum and two fat arbor-vitae plants on either side of the front door were the "in" thing in those days—but so was the Depression. She made the most of what was at hand—native and free for the taking—and I've noticed in the years since the 1930s that more knowledgeable and far grander gardeners do the same.

THERE ARE TIMES in the most garden-oriented life when you are distracted by other things and don't think much about cultivating the earth. One of these is when you are coming of age, falling in love and getting married. Looking back to that period in my life I realize that I wasn't completely oblivious to gardens and gardening. How could you be in Mobile, Alabama, that city of dreaming old gardens where azaleas are so old and so big that grownups picnic in their shade and small children caper in their branches like monkeys? I saw wonderful gardens every day, private ones and such celebrated ones as Mr. and Mrs. Walter D. Bellingrath's fishing-camp collection of pretties which had just begun to be professionally landscaped and gone "public".

As a young newspaper reporter I spent days down at the Bellingraths' every spring, writing stories about the expansion of the gardens and each new addition. I met my first professional landscape architect there. Mr. Bellingrath had asked him to show me around and explain the work to me. It was a priceless opportunity for me to have learned something but I guess I wasn't a very apt pupil. One of the first questions I asked him pegged me as almost irremediably ignorant.

"What," I asked, "is a vista?"

Beds and borders I knew about but a vista — an on-purpose view — golly!

Vistas didn't have much to do with my first personal garden. It was a fence-enclosed scrap of lawn beside a

garage apartment which my new husband and I rented overlooking Pensacola Bay. We could keep the grass cut with two swipes of the lawn mower but our predecessors in the apartment had marked off a foot-wide border around the fence and I found you could buy zinnias and marigold plants for a penny apiece from a housewife across town, known to all of us young marrieds as "the flower lady." We planted these and an occasional tomato plant among them and they did so well I decided to branch out. I would have sweet peas on the fence.

Sweet peas, my neighbors told me, didn't flourish in the salt wind and sandy soil. Besides, you had to plant them in the fall, months before you could expect any results, and for a working woman living in a rented place it was a lot of bother.

We bothered. We dug a trench and seasoned the sandy soil well with cow manure and leaf mold and watered in the big rough seeds. Nobody told me that they should have been soaked or frozen or notched so it was months before I saw my first sprig of green. I came home from work one chilly, windy afternoon—alone because my husband worked the night shift at the Pensacola News-Journal and late because I had swung by the doctor's office on my way. There, marching around the wire fence of our scrappy little yard was a brave bold battalion of tiny green plants.

We were going to have sweet peas—and a baby! I knelt down on the grass for a closer look at my plants and suddenly the excitement, the promise, the richness of life overwhelmed me. I cried like a fool.

Chapter 2

"The sweat that runs down the spade handle is the secret ingredient."

— Ken Kraft in *Gardener, Go Home!*

HEAVEN KNOWS THERE are plenty of expert gardeners in the world with a string of degrees in the plant sciences after their names and what Janet Gillespie in *Peacock Manure and Marigolds* called a "Lord and Taylored up" garden to prove it. They are right to make no secret of their expertise. They light the way for the likes of me — happy, bumbling duffers.

But I've noticed a modesty, a becoming reticence even in these members of the gardening fraternity. They know they have some knowledge. They have tested and proved their skills. But they also know that they do not work alone, that they can do their best, working hand in glove with the earth and the weather and there's still an element of chance, a touch of suspense about the results. Science and experience and hard work can do much with the earth but the mystery, the blessed mystery, remains.

Some garden writer (it could have been the great V. Sackville-West) once wrote, "Green thumb? Nonsense!" I came upon that prowling around in the library and I was pondering it, half believing but still questioning, when my neighbor Maude Miles amplified it for me with a bit of country wisdom she picked up from a farm woman for whom everything seemed to grow.

Good gardening, this woman told Maude, is not luck or witchcraft but it is very akin to prayer. You must first do everything you know to do to get the results you seek (lift that spade, tote that bale of peat and manure!) and when you have set the stage for success you must believe.

"You've got to have faith," the country woman said simply.

I must confess that when it comes to gardening I have always been long on hope but short on faith. By the house in the city where I lived for the longest time and brought up my three children I regularly planted seeds in the most unlikely places. There were too many shade trees, too many hungry tree roots, not enough fertility in the soil. Blithely I scattered seeds and blithely pronounced a curse on them: "Wouldn't it be lovely _if_ . . . ?"

That "if" was the tip-off, bespeaking both the uncertainty of the conditions and my faith.

Once, mostly for the entertainment of my mother who was visiting at the time, I put on a straw hat and gardening gloves, picked up a basket and clippers and went to the back yard for the morning rite she always called "doing the flowers." The fact that I brought back one sickly daisy of my own and two snapdragons surreptitiously fished through the hedge from my neighbor's yard made Muv laugh a little but with love and pity. She hated to see her only child a failure in a field so important to heart's ease and health in a mostly troubled and precarious world.

Later I learned that I could grow wild ferns, mountain laurel and rhododendron in that sour city soil and shade and I reluctantly gave up the idea of vegetables and brilliant blossoming borders that would fill the bowls and vases and baskets in the house. A lady who sold bunches of zinnias for thirty-five cents each outside the A&P on Saturdays continued to be my source of flowers for the house.

Then Sweet Apple came into my life—a funny little log cabin in a still predominantly rural settlement thirty miles from downtown Atlanta and my job and, as I kept assuring everybody, "with *sun*!"

When we uprooted and hauled away the dead plum thicket and junglelike tangle of honeysuckle that almost hid the old log house from the road the first thing we did sent my writing friend, Betsy Fancher, into stitches.

"You *didn't* call in a landscape architect!" howled Betsy as we walked over the yard and she saw the little one-room cabin looking as exposed as a picked chicken there on its teetering rock pillars with paneless windows gaping, its back door sagging and its front door grown shut.

"Yes, I did," I said with what dignity I could muster. "Edith Henderson herself. She was given to me for my birthday and she came."

For some reason getting a landscape architect for one's birthday was almost as funny to Betsy as having consulted her about this dreary and dilapidated patch of earth. But Mrs. Henderson herself had assured me that it was not a bit extraordinary. Since landscape architects charge by the hour for the quick and casual consultation, people frequently give their married children, new home owners and beginning gardeners, an hour or two of this expert counsel as a housewarming present. (I was later to give my daughter Susan and her husband an hour of Edith's time as a Christmas present. Edith made up a gift certificate and I tied it with red ribbon and tucked it into a basket with a book on flower arranging, some needlepoint holders, floral clay and a vase or two. It was one of my better Christmas ideas.)

The day Mrs. Henderson first came to Sweet Apple we seemed so remote and unreachable I felt it necessary to go four or five miles to the last paved crossroads to meet her. I needn't have bothered. She is a small and feminine person with fluffy silver hair and pink cheeks but fearless and competent and completely at home with old wagon roads, pock-marked flora and scraggly depleted fields that somebody yearns to turn into Eden. She stepped out of the car wearing jeans and sneakers and carrying a notebook and in no time at all she had walked over the ground, viewed the cabin from every angle and begun to make little sketches in her notebook.

Some of the things we did at once. Some, never. (She says it is ever thus.) We made a rock stoop at the front door, at her suggestion, instead of a full-fledged front porch which I had been thinking about. She drew in a trellis over the door with Carolina jessamine, which blooms beautifully in the spring and is evergreen, spilling over it.

She visualized a brick terrace on the chimney side of the house where there's shade in the afternoon, almost always a summer breeze and a pleasant view of the woods beyond. Her sketch curved the brickwork to allow room for the clump of old peach trees which we had pruned and fertilized and counted on for morning shade rather than fruit. Plant ajuga under the trees, she said, and build another trellis of poles from the woods to screen the terrace from the road. Before it plant six Golden Bell forsythias and on it plant three yellow jessamines for later. Immediately moonflowers, which I had been yearning for, would provide quick cover.

She suggested boxwood for the front corners of the cabin and I whooped at the idea. Boxwood seemed to me to be a cavalier kind of shrub, at home in the ordered gardens of old Virginia but lately taken up by suburbanites and altogether too flossy for a rude wilderness-type cabin.

"Look around you," suggested Edith.

And I began to.

The truth is that the pioneer settlers who came over the mountains from Virginia and the Carolinas brought with them roots and cuttings and seeds from the same things that had been brought over from the old gardens of England. Nearly every weathered mountain cabin or farmstead in the area boasts one or two gigantic boxwoods. My neighbors down the road, Paul and Jettie Belle Johnson, have one so tall it reaches the roof of their porch and nobody has any idea how old it is.

It was my first lesson in the democracy of plants. What is snooty and exotic and expensive beyond reach this year becomes, through the fraternity of garden sharing, at home in the poor man's patch next year. I have one friend, Mrs. Crawford Ware, an Englishwoman settled in

Hogansville, Georgia, who specializes in tracking down fine old French roses, sweet English violets and other ancient and elegant plants around abandoned home sites and through the pages of our state-published farm bulletin. It's not hard to believe when you talk to her that what grew in Marie Antoinette's garden in the eighteenth century flourishes today beside the smokehouse of a crude Appalachian cabin.

So I got the boxwood Edith suggested (a Christmas gift that very year) and also the dogwoods (another Christmas gift), which she visualized in a zigzag line across the front yard.

"I want roses on the fence," I said wistfully. "Yellow roses. And plenty of larkspur and cornflowers."

She drew me in a post and rail fence (I had one briefly but it rotted down) and spaced six Peace climbers at intervals along it.

As for larkspur and cornflowers, why just plant them in drifts along the fence, she said. Get several packages of seed and scatter them freely, one package at the time, along there where the yard slopes to the road.

We were to plant wild strawberries on the slope itself, transferring the bountiful supply from the yard where I wanted grass to the eroded bank, but that was one of the plans that never materialized. There are a few strawberries there through their own initiative but sumac and goldenrod and Queen Anne's lace moved in and I never had the heart to move them out. Besides, they served the useful purpose of turning some of the dust from the road.

The roses and drifts of larkspur and cornflowers

seemed a hopeless dream for a while. Simple and easy for other people but the minute I hear, "You can't miss. Just throw it on the ground and forget it," I know it will operate for me like some rare exotic that demands to be fed on ground-up diamonds and watered with the blood of pure white doves.

Larkspur . . . I planted them faithfully fall and spring. No luck. Cornflowers grew wild in fence rows and abandoned dooryards down the road. But the minute I scattered seeds in a freshly dug, richly fertilized bed they vanished. Roses? An exclusive club that blackballed me at every meeting.

And then suddenly my luck seemed to be changing. Not spectacularly and maybe not for keeps. But change it has. I have a rosebush that bloomed by the back steps faithfully for three or four years. It's not what it was labeled when I bought it — the old yellow Maréhal Niel of my mother's garden — but a nameless little pink semiclimber that gives me a bloom or two almost every day between April and October. Not enough to set a rosarian's pulses hammering, I know, but one of its blooms on the table in a rose-painted cream pitcher or an old gold-rimmed hatpin holder (if the stem is long) makes me feel like a millionaire when I sit down to breakfast.

So heartened was I by owning a rosebush with the will to live (the Peaces expired on the front fence) that I planted eight new ones last winter. (Three of them were gifts from neighbors whose Pink Spices turned me green with shameful, obvious covetousness.) Almost always there's a bud or two coming or a fat fully opened blossom going. Even my neighbor Betsy Hastings, who married into the self-same seedsmen family my mother used to "order off" from and has a proper rose garden, agrees that to have one rose at a time can really be riches enow.

Sometimes I think that a plump Constance Spry bouquet of roses with buds and blooms falling all over each other will be mine someday but I don't really care. In our summer heat cut roses start drooping almost the minute you bring them indoors and an opulent bouquet would seem a waste. Dorothy Parker can be as derisive as she likes about "one perfect rose":

> *Why is it no one ever sent me yet*
> *One perfect limousine, do you suppose?*
> *Ah, no, it's always just my luck to get*
> *One perfect rose.*

That one perfect dew-spangled bud for the breakfast table . . . I'll settle for it any day.

WITH CORNFLOWERS AND LARKSPUR there was also a turning point. Larkspur planted last fall, new seeds from the store and old seeds from a volunteer my neighbor Mrs. Cora Stewart gave me, sprang up in great green virility in the early spring and I never saw such a lush stand of cornflowers in my life. All during April I kept going out and examining them to make sure they weren't weeds. I had been ready to renounce larkspur forever when Mrs. Stewart called up one night and said she had "oodlings" of plants, some she was going to pull up and throw away to make room for something else. I could have all I wanted.

Another neighbor, Verda Smellie, no mean gardener herself, went with me to the lovely blooming dooryard two old people in their eighties, Miss Cora and Mr. Shawdie, cultivate around a house as aged as my 1842 log cabin. Everything there was old and hardy and blooming profligately, tumbling over a rock wall, climbing up trellises, nudging the protruding roots of shade trees and filling borders and beds with a riot of color.

Verda wasn't optimistic about my chances of getting a stand of larkspur from such sizable plants yanked summarily from a bed. Even when you plant their seed in little peat pots and tenderly transfer pot and all to the bed you get only so-so results, she said. But Mrs. Stewart, who tends a vast vegetable garden, cooks, cans, freezes, fishes and raises fishworms for sale, handles her flowers with a casual ease and optimism that brooks no failure.

"Don't worry," she said, handing me a newspaper wad of ten-inch tall plants. "Stick them in the ground, shade them for a few days and give them plenty of water and you'll have larkspur all right." And I have.

All of which causes me to conclude that, in truth, you do have to believe. But you better prepare the soil first and if there's any magic, witchcraft or plain blind luck going your way, grab it, too.

Chapter 3

"In order to live OFF a garden, a man practically has to live IN it."

— Kin Hubbard

IT'S FUNNY HOW LONG it takes you to see a perfectly obvious thing. For the first half-dozen years in the country I wanted a big garden and everything I had ever heard about to be growing in it — the delicate spring lettuces, endive, escarole and romaine, radishes and tender young peas, new potatoes and all the summer vegetables — black-eyed peas and butter beans, okra, squash, tomatoes and great purple eggplant. I saw no reason why I couldn't have strawberries and asparagus and blueberries and raspberries and blackberries and grapes and watermelons and cucumbers and cantaloupe.

In winter, of course, I would have sweet potatoes banked under domes of earth and straw somewhere back there in the woods. I would, of course, have to get from my neighbor Mr. Lum Crow the nearest grist mill's schedule, for, naturally, I would be taking my corn there to have it converted into grits and meal.

The plain truth was that although I had the space— five acres mostly given over to young pines and hard-woods—I had neither the time nor the help to handle a big garden. My husband died while we still lived in town, the children had grown up and married and weren't close by. I had a newspaper job with hours that while flexible could sometimes run long and involve out-of-town travel.

If I could get the garden plowed—and at first I had to call on my tractor-owning neighbors for this at their busiest time of year—I sometimes wouldn't be at home at the proper time to plant it. Baskets full of unplanted seeds reproached me at the end of every season. And there was always the problem of watering and weeding. By the first of July my little garden spot was the settle-ment's show place of lusty, strapping weeds, bound and gagged and draped and festooned with a glorious crop of purple and blue morning glories. (It sometimes gave me a little wry satisfaction to think of the weeds as giant Gullivers and the morning glories as Lilliputians pinion-ing and staking them to the ground. Both were so pesky.) If I had beans and tomatoes—and ah, I did have beans and tomatoes!—I couldn't find them for the devil's shoe-string and dock.

There was the problem of flowers. I wanted them. I was determined to have them. But there's a dour Cal-vinistic streak in me that makes me feel guilty about fiddling around with daisies if the butter beans are parch-ing in their pods for want of water. The food crop came first with my country ancestors and it came first with me.

There was grass—of sorts—to mow in front of the cabin and although I am not giddy about an impeccable greensward, you have to keep it in abeyance or it will rise up and choke you. And that takes time.

The terrace Edith Henderson sketched for me had been built and the forsythia and jessamine were growing so well they made an almost see-through-proof green wall between me and the road. It was a terrible temptation to sit there and read and sip coffee before work in the mornings and to sit there and sip something cool and visit with friends in the late afternoons but how could I with that disheveled, sun-baked garden standing there shaming me for my neglect?

The woods drew me, too. One of the reasons I moved to the country was to be near the woods, to take long walks, to sit on a hill under a tree and look at the sky, to maybe fish or swim a little. I had wildflower books and a passionate desire to find and identify and possibly even collect a few of practically everything that bloomed. But the bed for asparagus needed digging and there was fertilizer to haul. Wasn't anybody going to do anything about that shaggy gray stuff that grew on the apple tree?

"There just isn't TIME enough!" I used to wail to anybody who would listen.

And then I remembered Mary Kistner and her one-woman garden.

Mary and her husband, David, were city people who bought a big five hundred-acre farm and started raising pure-bred cattle near Lawrenceville. They were friends of friends of mine and the first time I went by to see them I was completely captivated by a pocket-handkerchief-sized vegetable garden at the corner of the back lawn.

There was a variety of vegetables but a small amount of each thing with herbs and flowers — *not* weeds — intermingled and the whole thing looking as diminutive and perky and eye-catching as a Victorian nosegay.

"It's so *small*!" I cried to Mary and she took me around and showed me that it was indeed small, tailored to supply fresh vegetables in season for two people and occasional guests. That was all. None to can, preserve or freeze, none to dry up or decay on the vine. Just *enough*.

She had to plan it that way, said Mary, because the task of raising and marketing pure-bred cattle was a full-time job for David and there was no other labor she could call on. Once a year he helped her get her garden going and after that she was on her own.

She had worked out a system, probably after a little period for trial and error, that gave her time for other activities but assured that in the growing season she would always have fresh vegetables for the table, herbs to season them and flowers to ornament the yard and garnish the rooms of the old and handsomely restored farmhouse. And her garden looked so neat and healthy.

"Plenty of cow manure, a lively compost pile and mulch," said Mary.

In spite of knowing about Mary Kistner's one-woman garden I didn't think of trying to trim mine to conform to the limits of my own time and strength until I read Ruth Stout's *How to Have a Green Thumb Without an Aching Back*. She and her husband moved to the country with the understanding that neither would expect the other to help or interfere with his particular project. The garden was her project and she was strongly committed to the

principle that no one should lift a finger in it "unless he loved doing it."

It suddenly struck me as eminently sound logic with a touch of the spiritual. After all, a garden is a creative undertaking much like writing a poem or painting a picture and if you have to whine around begging, cajoling and paying people to help you it's no good. If they *love* it and want to help that's a different matter. And if you could hire somebody to do some of the heavier earth-moving, back-breaking jobs of getting ready to garden, it would be fine. But you seldom *can* any more, so it makes sense to limit your project to what you and sympathetic friends and relatives (if they show up) can manage.

With that in mind I went out and looked at my patch again. It wasn't big—about forty feet long by thirty-five feet wide, running from a couple of mulberry trees and the corncrib on the east to the apple tree on the west, facing the house on the north and the woods on the south. My neighbor Jack Strong and I had admired the neat pebbled paths in a Williamsburg-like garden back of a restored Revolutionary War vintage house when we visited it once. (It has since been moved to make way for the new big Arts Center.) With him to do the digging and shoveling, we laid a tidy pebbled path to and through my garden.

Nobody told me that pebbles not only don't discourage grass and weeds but that they stimulate and nurture them. So it was no time at all before my pebble walk was springy and green with grass and weeds. I had seen sod walks in English gardens, so the answer seemed to be to mow it and forget the pebbles.

Now if my garden was to be a one-woman, trowel-and-hoe operation it seemed a good idea to take another tuck in it and make another path. We did, with the result that there are four beds for flowers about eighteen feet long and four feet wide each. Paths, which I try to run the mower over once a week, separate them from each other and from the remaining two plots, about fifteen by sixteen feet each, which are reserved for vegetables, except along the edges where I have stuck in herbs and flowers, mostly zinnias for cutting and marigolds for their happy faculty of repelling insect pests.

Two more beds are a-building. The cow manure piled in the last sunny space before the woods begin marks the site where there will be one long bed for asparagus and the same, on the other side of the path, for strawberries — both of them raised if I can wangle enough crossties to do it. These crops, strawberries and asparagus, had a go at life in the original garden patch and after an earnest effort to show me something, evidence decided the traffic and the competition were too great and gave up. I believe they will like their own bailiwick better, especially if it is lavishly furnished with the finest from my neighbor Denver Corn's barnyard.

Once I had settled on the size and shape of the garden, whacking away at weeds as I thought about it, my neighbor Jack brought over a rototiller and gave the earth what I hope will be its last all-out, all-over turning. I raked away as many grass and weed roots as I could find, we hauled in lime, cottonseed meal and cow manure and applied it with a free hand to each of the beds and covered the whole thing with hay snatched out of the mouths of Erle Miles's cows. (Spoiled hay would have been just as well for this, maybe even better, but we missed the 25-cents-a-bale bargain we saw advertised on a sign on the fence of a horse farm down the road and I was impatient to begin and didn't want to take the time to look farther.)

Erle's pastures lying along Little River are so green most of the year he felt his cows could spare me a few bales of hay and that's what we got. When that ran out I brought in pine straw, oak leaves and grass clippings and sawdust from the old sawmill site down in the woods. I haven't quite achieved the eight-inch mulch advocated by Ruth Stout, but what I have added has helped to keep vegetables and flowers green and thrifty during the worst of the summer drought and has discouraged, if not defeated, the weeds.

The total effect is not Mary Kistner's flawless little Eden with smartly mitered corners and everything blossoming and bearing in joyous roundelay. But it looks better than it ever has. The butter peas are swelling in their purse-shaped pods, the late tomatoes are up to my eyebrows, growing taller and loaded with fruit, and the early tomato patch, newly cleared last week and scattered with a medley of seeds — turnips, mustard, beets and a sprinkling of radishes to repel bugs — is greening up fast.

It's true that there are weeds but not as many as usual and much easier to wrest from the mulched earth. (That softness and ease under the moist mulch gets to even the invincible Johnson grass. Instead of plunging its big tough tuberlike roots halfway to China it lets them loll around in cushiony comfort near the surface.)

The grass from my walks eludes the mower along the edges and sneaky runners trespass into flower and vegetable precincts but an hour with clippers and edger will

take care of most of that and next year...ah, *next year!*
This looking ahead, this planning and the occasional flash
of vision probably constitute the best thing in a gardener's
life. For as Miles and John Hadfield wrote in *Gardens of
Delight,* "Fundamentally, all gardening is the transference
or a vision into a touchable and seeable reality."

Chapter 4

"Americans must be far more brotherly-hearted than we are, for they do not seem to mind being overlooked. They have no sense of private enclosure."

—V. Sackville-West

AMATEUR GARDENERS need all the confidence they can get and the best device I know for shoring up one's belief in one's own aspirations, if not achievements, is to seek out the authorities. Just as they say the devil can quote scripture for his own evil purposes (they do say that, don't they?), it's possible for the fledgling gardener to find some expert to advocate whatever he wants to do.

Take thickets. I love thickets. I love being enclosed by walls of green growing things. I have not the slightest desire to see or be seen by the people passing my door on the dirt road. In fact, it seems to me that one of the great needs of the human spirit nowadays is for privacy—a spot of earth where you can be alone.

Time was, I know, when aloneness was the condition of country living and not too desirable. My predecessors at Sweet Apple had to fight their way through a wilderness to get here and a symbol of home was a clearing—a little space where you could see the approach of enemy or friend, a swept area wild animals would be reluctant to cross, a clean spot where even the smallest snake track would be visible. The landscaping in those days didn't include foundation planting, which is to say flowers and shrubs around the walls of the cabin. Whatever ornamental bushes and trees the householder got were set off at a distance. Boxwood, if any, grew in the middle of the yard. The old clump of mock orange which was here when I came was up the slope and halfway to the garden.

The cabin itself was built close to the road—for company, I suppose, as well as for convenience. Transportation was difficult at best and people wanted to be as near to the public roads as possible. If anybody passed, the family with no telephone or automobile wanted to be at least within hailing distance. Even better, the passing traveler might stop and share a bed or a meal and relate all the news from the world beyond.

The need to be near passing traffic no longer exists but habit is strong. People who have small lots necessarily build cheek by jowl to their neighbors. But even with space to spare you'll see new houses going up, all barefaced and exposed, next to the paved road. And then when the craving for privacy hits, you'll see a redwood-enclosed patio going up in the back.

The style for the "uncluttered" came along a few years ago and throughout the land you saw householders taking down picket fences and the wonderful old iron fences. They uprooted their hedges, whacked down their dark cedars and hauled away old and fat ligustrum bushes.

(And a good thing that last was, too!) The fashion was for sweeps of unblemished lawn and maybe a few low-growing hollies around the eaves to sort of anchor the house to the land. (I had a friend who planted the thorn-iest holly she could find under all her windows to repel burglars.)

Everybody in the world went crazy about sun and the old passion for shade trees — for elm- and oak-lined streets — languished. With air conditioners humming away at every window, who needed trees to cool the air and shade the roof? We all spoke feelingly of openness and light and the joys of having the sun shine in our windows.

There were holdouts, of course, and my mother, Muv, was one of them. When everybody else in her little town took down their fences on the ground that there was no longer any wandering livestock in the streets, Muv painted hers and trained a wisteria along its top runner. When her neighbors, lately come from yards hard swept with gallberry brush brooms, went in for wide and treeless lawns, Muv cut swatches out of hers to allot to a magnolia tree, a new water oak, a mimosa, a jackaranda, a tea olive and assorted beds and borders of azaleas, camellias and roses. Further offending the eyes of her neighbors, she planted a screen of vines and bridal wreath stage center so she would have a hiding place to sit unseen and sip her coffee in the early morning.

Newcomers to her street made the mistake of think-ing Muv lived in this jungle because she was getting along in years and lacked the strength to prune. So when she went to the hospital for a few days once they gener-ously got together and trimmed up her trees and leveled her bushy tangle of coral vines and bridal wreath to the ground.

It suited me very well not to be present when they came for their thanks.

By the time I got there she had replanted. The result is not one to gladden the eye of a landscape architect and draw photographers from House & Garden magazine, but it is right for Muv and her birds and her cats.

When she wanders forth with her coffee in the mornings she has, even on her smallish lot, some place to go, something to see. There are crooks and turns, little paths to follow, minute views to surprise the eye. You don't take it all in at once. There's a small patch of open lawn big enough for a bird bath and a feeder but not so big it taxes the strength of the man who comes twice a month to cut the grass for her. There are caverns of coolness beneath the bushes for her cats and a bench here or a chair there for Muv to rest upon.

Oddly enough, the crowding doesn't seem an impediment to most of Muv's plants. The pomegranate tree by the kitchen wall puts out blazing flowers all summer and an occasional harvest of fruit. Her tea olive by the screened porch sweetens the late winter and early spring air with its fragrance and a magnolia between her and her neighbor's fence perfumes the late spring and summer. Defying all the rules for growing roses as to spacing and pruning, Muv still manages to have something blooming all the time. Her camellias are a wonder and when all else peters out quantities of lilies lift pristine, gold-filled cups above an untidy green snarl of foliage, their own and other plants'.

Naturally, being a child of the uncluttered garden era, I didn't plan to emulate my mother's jungle. The first thing I did at Sweet Apple was to skin the front yard bare of everything except four spindly pine saplings, a seedling peach and one wild plum. Then we set about planting grass, wonderful grass. The winter rye popped up promptly, looking in sere November like a lush carpet of artificial green spread by an unctuous undertaker to hide an honest grave. I really hated that glorious, phony greensward but comforted myself that it was nurturing the earth and, come spring, we would plant real grass that would be green only in season and decently brown in season.

Whatever we planted — and I mercifully forgot — was all wrong. It languished and died. Manure was needed, we

decided, and enlisted the services of Herb Hawkins, whose family runs a Roswell seed-feed store. One hot summer day young Mr. Hawkins arrived in a mighty truck equipped with a fan, which blew chicken litter all over the yard. Back and forth he drove and what my son called "the material" hit the fan and then the yard.

Anybody who has smelled chicken litter — the stuff that comes from the floor of the chicken houses — under the hot Georgia sun will comprehend my dedication to the dream of a good lawn. The idea, Mr. Hawkins said, was to get it out before the rain. It would, he admitted, smell a little until we had a good rain to wash the rich and pungent scent into the earth.

That was the understatement of the century. That chicken litter stank. It was not a mildly offensive odor that you could sniff and forget. It was a stench, oppressive, pervasive, overpowering.

And that was the summer it didn't rain.

One night my son, Jimmy, and I drove into the yard from town and the aroma of chicken litter reached out and got us not just strong enough to scorch our noses but strong enough to craze the enamel on the car.

It was hot and we knew we would have to sleep with the windows open. Sleep? We'd be asphyxiated!

The impulse hit us simultaneously. We rushed in and grabbed up some blankets and headed north to camp out. The mountain camp was eighty miles away but at that point eighty miles seemed scarcely far enough.

Eventually, of course, it rained and time and the weather dissipated the chicken litter. The grass began to grow and so did the weeds. My dream of a velvet stretch of uncluttered lawn went a-glimmering. I had chick weed, dock, plantain, dandelions and thousands of other little wildings that were nameless to me. At first our neighbor Doc comforted me by saying that it was all green and if you kept it cut who was to know that it wasn't grass?

But keeping weeds mowed is harder than keeping grass mowed. They are not content to creep along the earth but must reach for the sky and I guess they have more dominant personalities than effete, citified, cultivated grass blades. Anyhow, with a resignation born of desperation, I began to look, really look, at those weeds and they began to strike me as more interesting than grass.

For one thing, most weeds are herbs and are good for

something. You can't make a poultice or a tea with grass. At least, I never heard that you could. But weeds...ah, country lore is full of stories about their magical healing properties. Cocklebur, for instance, can be steeped in a tea, sweetened with honey and served up for sore and husky throats. (One ounce of dried leaves to one pint of boiling water, honey to taste, an old herbal says.)

Ground ivy, the tenacious little plant with the sharp, aromatic odor, filled me with despair when it got in flower beds and spilled over and snuffed out grass, until I read that the scent of its crushed foliage inhaled deeply will cure headaches when all other efforts have failed. It is also good for poultices for "abcesses, gatherings and tumours" and valued by gypsies for making ointments for cuts or sprains. Now I leave it where it grows and enjoy the scent it gives off when I walk or push the lawn mower over it.

Plantain, which took a stand in my yard, sending big turnipy roots down to China, didn't look at all ornamental to me until I learned its other name is "Englishman's foot." This is said to have been given to it by the Indians because it seemed to spring up everywhere the white man went. Romeo in Romeo and Juliet recommended it "for your broken shin" and all sorts of authorities have found use for it in poultices to draw out poison, in infusions for diarrhea and ointments for sore eyes.

But you really can't turn your front yard into a weed patch without offending the taste of all your neighbors and any random passerby. Which brings me back to the need of privacy. A woman's log cabin should be her castle and she should feel free, even comfortable, to have a lawn, mown or unmown, a weed patch or a jungle, if it suits her. I wouldn't go so far as to say she could have a fence made of old tires painted silver or a gate of old bedsteads. But on the other hand, if she wanted such in her yard and kept it hidden from the general view...?

It was a very appealing idea to me and I talked about it off and on for years but rather hopelessly. Sweet Apple is close to the road and traffic is increasing every day. A dozen new houses have been built within two miles of us within the last eight years and 75 others are going up in the beautiful pasture three miles away. Time will come when a respectable woman dare not wander around in the cool of the evening in her shimmy or sit under a tree in her pajamas to drink her morning coffee.

The pines in the front yard were growing, of course, and three of the nine dogwoods that we planted in a zigzag line across the front had plumped out. When the road crews stopped hacking it back we turned out to have quite a nice stand of sumac and an old crape myrtle tree that some long-ago owner planted here. The Dorothy

Perkins rose ran rampant over the yard and into the trees before we cleared it out and threw it on the road bank. Now it runs rampant on the road bank and sprawls all over the rail fence, offering bouquets of pink shattery blooms for about two weeks out of the year and growing, growing, growing the rest of the time. In summer there are blackberries and Queen Anne's lace and daisies to turn the dust; in the fall, goldenrod. On the whole, an unsightly mess, my family and friends tell me, and why don't I clear it away and plant grass?

Lacking the courage of my convictions, I didn't shout, "Never!" or even try to defend my burgeoning fence row. That is, I didn't until I found my authority.

In her book, *A Joy of Gardening*, V. Sackville-West has this to say about the advantages of a thicket. She says the American attitude of "All is open. Walk in, walk in!" probably illustrates an admirable democratic spirit but it isn't likely to be emulated in Britain.

"It is entirely at variance with our traditional idea that our own bit of ground surrounding our house, our home, be it large or small, is sacred to ourselves," she writes.

So the plan, advanced by an acquaintance, of going beyond planting "a mere hedge" and planting a thicket strikes her as "a very useful idea."

"Thickets," she points out, "can be planted any-where, can be of any shape, and can be composed of any plants to your choice. If I had room for a thicket myself and had enough span of life to look forward to it twenty years hence, I know what I should do: I should plant it far too thickly and extravagantly to start with, and then should thin it gradually as my shrubs and trees developed in size, crowding one another out.... You could remove, and add, and alter, indefinitely. There would be no end to the fun and interest and variety."

I have never been to Sissinghurst Castle but I have a feeling Miss Sackville-West's estate is at least slightly bigger than mine and anybody would say that she had more room for a thicket. But no matter. The need for a thicket can live in the heart of a log cabin dweller as well as in the heart of the chatelaine of an English castle.

It's the privacy that we covet, the sense of being enclosed by greenness, secure from the public gaze. If V. Sackville-West says a thicket is horticulturally sound and esthetically proper, who's to answer nay?

So, emboldened by my authority, I have embarked on my thicket. You can have free rein in dreaming up a thicket. (The planting is a bit more difficult.) How about holly trees? A weeping willow? More dogwood? Sourwood, that gem of a little tree that is laden with panicles of white beloved by the bees all summer and a blazing bonfire of brilliant, lacquered red in the fall? Althea, the little summer-blooming tree whose other name is Rose of Sharon? You could plant more sumac. That exotic-looking wilding called "shoemake" in the rural South is handsome with its stag horns of deep red berries and its flaming autumnal foliage. There are shrubs — all the viburnmums, wild azaleas, sweet shrub, mock orange.

How about a crab apple tree for springtime fragrance and heart-stopping pink blossoms?

All the experts not in accord with your yearning for a thicket will tell you that these trees and bushes need space. They will warn you to visualize the grown tree and allow room accordingly. I have but to look out my window at one of nature's thickets and know that they are not necessarily right. I see pines and young maples, dogwood, hickories, sweetgums and wild plums clumped together, making an impenetrable wall to the west of me. Why not in front?

An artist friend warned me that it would spoil the view of Sweet Apple cabin from the road but from the inside looking out, what could be pleasanter than a thicket, a real thick thicket?

Now when opposition arises I do what I advise all neophyte gardeners to do. I drop a name: "V. Sackville-West says..."

Chapter 5

"Some people say, 'Shoot an organic gardener and you'll kill a nut'..."

— Ken Kraft

IT'S BEEN MY PAIN AND PLEASURE in many years of newspapering to have known a lot of crusaders. I have seen — and sometimes joined — fighters for everything from planned parenthood to banned fireworks. The first heady crusade I mounted as a fifteen-year-old summer vacation reporter on the Mobile Press involved getting milk, ice to keep it and diapers for six newborn babies. The magic in the old newspaper dictum "Let the people know" was so overwhelming that I still haven't recovered from it.

Drop a catch phrase — "Save the Marshlands!" "Get Out the Vote!" "Treat Sick Alcoholics!" — and I gird myself for battle.

And yet, as a young friend of mine once pointed out after a particularly exhausting session with one set of saviors (they were either for or against abortions, I forget which): "Good people are very fatiguing."

They are. Even when their cause is just—and it so often is—they get so swept away by their missionary zeal they can't talk or think of anything else. No matter how persuasive they are at first, how profound and stirring their arguments, before they are done with their subject their listeners are glaze-eyed with boredom and exhaustion.

Organic gardeners are not immune to this malady of the species zealot. They will talk the ears off anybody they can hogtie into listening. They will bombard the unwary with tracts. They shudder and grow loud and abusive on the subject of chemical fertilizers and poison dusts and sprays. Their eyes burn with a holy zeal and their voices grow husky with emotion when they speak of compost, natural manures and companionate planting.

There's one old gentleman, a whale of a composter, who regularly leaves on my desk sacks of rich dark loamy

soil laced with earthworms—just to remind me, in case I'm ever tempted to backslide, that this is The Way. I value the attention—and the compost—but it isn't necessary now. I am a convert or, at least as King Agrippa told the apostle Paul, I am almost persuaded.

At first I wasn't. The time-tested method of my country neighbors seemed good enough for me. They invested a lot in nitrate of soda. (The cost of "sody" and guano used to keep the poor southern tenant farmer in bondage to the company store.) They plowed and replowed the earth to break up the hard clay and to get rid of the weeds. They fought garden pests from A to Z— or A, aphids, to W, wireworms, anyhow. They used every poison spray and dust that came on the market. Their results seemed thoroughly satisfactory to me.

Then I visited a friend who was so quiet about it I didn't even know she was an organic gardener. We walked out into her yard and the impact of one squash vine stunned me. From out of what looked like a mess of rubbish almost black-green squash vines swarmed all over the place with flowers as big as picture hats and exquisitely tender little golden squashes. Her okra, likewise proceeding from a snarl of straw, grass clippings and dead weed stalks, was a picture. Tomatoes lolled voluptuously over bales of hay and where the earth showed, black and velvety, it was stitched with a crisp green ruching of leaf lettuce.

As she dug me a clump of oregano to take home with me she answered my unspoken question with a smile.

"Yes, I'm one," she murmured.

"Organic?" I whispered, not wishing to set off a tirade.

"Um-m," she nodded.

"To the core."

I took the plunge.

"Would you let me see your compost pile?"

This is it," she said.

I didn't see anything that remotely resembled the composting venture I embarked on when I first owned a piece of land. It had been both my delight and my despair. I enjoyed piling up the leaves and there was something thrifty and housewifely about mixing in coffee grounds and egg shells and vegetable trimmings. But then I would forget to water the whole mess down or wasn't at home when it was time to turn it and although it produced marvelous fish bait for the boys in the family who were diligent enough to churn up the leaves and straw looking, it didn't ever reach that peak of loose, black, friable soil that the old gentleman brings me. His smells good. Mine smelled like garbage. By strict attention to those twin duties, turning and timing, he could convert anything—I suspect paper and tin cans included—into pure sweet earth in a matter of three or four weeks. Everything I plunked into my compost pile, and some things I didn't even remember putting there, sprouted. As that gardener-humorist Ken Kraft once remarked of his own composting endeavor, I should have paid an amusement tax.

And here was my organic gardening friend with no proper compost pile.

"What do you mean this is your compost pile?" I asked, feeling somehow betrayed. "What do you do with your egg shells?"

She turned aside a bit of straw with her toe. There nestled down next to a stand of beautiful beets was her day's collection of kitchen garbage—the morning grapefruit rinds cut into small pieces to hasten their return to the soil, coffee grounds, egg shells, bean pods and carrot tops and scrapings.

It was the same all over the garden. She kept a bowl on her kitchen counter and everything but scraps of cooked food, which she gave her pets, and grease went into it. At cleanup time she turned back the counterpane of mulch on her vegetable and flower beds and tucked in the organic garbage. It all breaks down just the same, maybe not as fast as that which is piled up and methodically watered and turned, but it's certainly quick and easy disposal and I've been doing the same for about a year now.

From time to time when my daughters or other visitors help with the cleaning up after a meal bits of bread and an occasional meaty bone will find its way into my counter compost trove. (I used to use a bowl covered with a plate but at a wayside teahouse in Devonshire I bought a tin Devon cream bucket with a bail and a lid and it's perfect by the sink.) When it happens that tidbits of food get in the garden there's always danger the dogs will scent it and start digging. For a while I patiently picked out anything, however small, that might attract them, but then my friend Julia Fitch, Roswell librarian and a good gardener, gave me a priceless tip. Pluck a few toadstools and toss them on the heap and the dogs won't go near it.

"It seems a dirty trick," said Julia, who likes dogs. "But it's quick and it works. They evidently know a poison mushroom, even if we don't, and they steer clear of them."

Natural fertilizers have always appealed to me. Not that they smell any better—neither is Chanel No. 5. But you can see that they improve the texture of the earth. The soil in my garden and most of the gardens in this area has a substantial base of that famed Georgia clay. It looks beautiful when it's plowed in the spring, running the gamut from pale yellow to peach to burnt orange and finally that deep plum red. But for a hundred years or more most of it was planted to cotton and when a horticulturist speaks of land as being "cottoned out" you know what he means. It looks naked and exposed and gets that tired and drained look that you've seen on the faces of sharecroppers' wives. Nothing was put back into the soil except guano in the spring. It baked and cracked under the summer sun and washed and ran red into gullies and creeks under heavy rains.

My little patch, once part of a big cotton farm, was no better except that the last people who lived in my cabin back in the 1930s kept a few chickens out there and in all the years it has been vacant weeds grew up and died and returned to the soil. So there was a layer of topsoil containing some organic matter. I determined that it should have more and every time I heard of somebody who had cow manure or chicken litter free for the hauling I organized work parties. Once my son brought his girl out for the weekend and I awakened her early Sunday morning with a clarion call.

"Come on!" I cried. "Jack has brought his truck and we're all going to Alpharetta!"

She didn't ask what was going on in Alpharetta, a little town six or eight miles to the east of us, and it must not have occurred to me to tell her. I don't think I was so unsporting as to deliberately conceal the nature of our mission. Anyhow, when I handed her the shovel in a dairyman's cow barn and commanded her to start loading the truck I noticed for the first time that she was wearing superbly tailored slacks, hand-sewn loafers and a cashmere sweater. She didn't whimper or try to beg off. She shoveled. (I always did like that girl.)

Out of every batch of cow manure I try to save some for what my mother calls "tea"—a dark brown liquid made from putting a sack of fertilizer in a barrel or drum of water and allowing it to steep. When Muv called, "Tea time!" in the late afternoon in Creola, Alabama, she didn't mean for us. She meant for her ferns and coleus and her tomato plants. She filled a bucket at the "tea barrel" and carefully and judiciously ladled it out, a dipperful at the time, to anything that looked the least bit "peaked."

The trouble with me and the natural fertilizers, of course, was that after hauling them and spreading them I expected to jump back and watch them do the rest. If I didn't step lively, I thought, I would be inundated by a lush green tide. I was. A lush green tide of weeds. Everything those cows and chickens had ever even looked at, much less eaten, came up in my garden and reached for the sky.

That was the reason, some of my neighbors told me gently, for using the commercial fertilizers. That powdery stuff you buy in sacks may not change the texture of your soil but it doesn't sprout weeds. I thought of changing. Those figures they print on the commercial fertilizer sacks (6-8-8, 8-10-12 and the like) are very seductive. They tell you how much sulphate, phosphate and lime you get for your money. With my standbys, cow manure and cottonseed meal, you have no figures to guide you. (I'm sure I trust cottonseed meal because it smells so terrible when it gets wet.)

Still, there was the example of my organic gardening friend before me and I hated to chicken out. I got some garden books, Jean Hersey's and Ruth Stout's among them, and there was the answer. Use the natural manures but choke the weeds out before they can lift their heads above ground by piling on the mulch. Mulch, mulch, mulch, they cried.

The happy thing about the organic gardeners' mulching tenet is that all the pros seem to be in accord with them on this. Fred Galle, immediate past president of the American Horticultural Society and horticulturist in charge of the famous Callaway Gardens at Pine Mountain, Georgia, told me that he is a miser about every bit of leaves, bark, weeds and straw that hits the ground in the 1500-acre area under his supervision. They have four upright silos for storage measuring 20 by 40 feet by 5 feet high, holding one hundred tons each. Black plastic covers the lot and more plastic collects the seepage from this organic pudding and pumps it back into the silos. It is turned frequently and when "done" it is mixed about half and half with the soil. He used to buy five or six hundred bales of peat a year but that is no longer necessary since the gardens' own composting operation is going. He does, however, keep the gardens' trucks busy hauling pine bark and sawdust from neighboring sawmills.

The land where the gardens now flourish was spent and worn when the founder, the late Cason J. Callaway, had his dream of making it "the most beautiful garden since Adam was boy." But you wouldn't know it now. The topsoil is dark and deep and friable and the unflagging succession of flowers, fruit, vegetables, cultivated and native shrubs and trees have made the Callaway Gardens famous throughout the country.

Aubrey Owens, president of the Georgia Horticultural Society and noted for his work in developing the old wild muscadine or bullace grape into a vineyard favorite throughout fourteen states, departed the "clean cultivation" system some time ago. Long before the U. S. Department of Agriculture came around to that view he had stopped plowing the rows between the vines in his vineyard and started mowing the weeds and grass. He allows the clippings to stay on the ground and is delighted that his vines are laying their own carpet of compost to shade and hold the moisture around their roots. He doesn't spray either but he does use commercial fertilizers for the reason that they are easy and available.

The only real differences between the trained professional horticulturists and the organic girls and boys (some of whom are well trained themselves) seem to be on the use of chemical fertilizers and poisons. Being an amateur with a great deal of respect for the work done by those people trained in the plant sciences I don't presume to say who is right. But I did read Rachel Carson's *The Silent Spring* and I haven't been able to pick up a pesticide or a weed killer since. And when I think of buying a quick and easy sack of commercial fertilizer I remember the garden of my friend Laura Dorsey.

Laura and her husband, Hugh, an Atlanta lawyer, have a country place in the adjoining county a few miles northwest of Sweet Apple. They live in the city but regularly spend weekends on the farm and Laura devotes one day in the middle of the week to it—with help, if she can hire it, or recruit volunteers among her family and friends, without help if necessary. The place is completely captivating.

The old house is one that used to be in Sweet Apple settlement. It was the home of our late neighbor Granny Reese. When she moved in with her children, Mr. and Mrs. Homer Dangar, the old log and clapboard homestead stood vacant. The Dorseys owned acreage in Cherokee County, including a hill with a view of the mountains—the perfect place, Laura knew at once, for an old house. When I first came to Sweet Apple the house had been sold and moved but people were still talking about how "little Mrs. Dorsey, that nice lady" personally took up her post in the middle of the public highway and routed traffic around the moving operation.

Today the house, its weathered silver gray walls and slanty roof unchanged, commands the view from a green hill with a lake at its feet, woods all around it, a sweep of grass with fruit trees, grapes and beehives in front and a beautiful vegetable garden behind it. Mint and herbs and such wildlings as trillium and bird's-foot violets grow cheek by jowl beside the kitchen door and bright red cannas march along the front of the house.

I saw their garden plot in the spring when they were planting it and again in late summer when the harvest was about over. The corn was gone and the stalks were drying, the squash had borne its last and Joan Law, a young friend who had come with Laura to help, was filling a bushel basket with what they thought might be the last of the tomatoes.

There were weeds to pull and drying vegetable stalks to uproot and lay aside to make way for the fall garden seeds Laura was in a hurry to get into the ground. But it wasn't hard work because of the deep layer of leaves and pine bark that covered everything. A slight yank and the weed or plant came up and was stowed lightly by the row where it had grown—everything, that is, except the tenacious Bermuda grass which Laura relentlessly banished. To plant new seeds she pushed back the mulch, sifted in a little dark ground granite dust, which a firm turns out near Stone Mountain and markets under the name of Hybrotite, and added her seeds.

Later as we sat in the kitchen over sandwiches and iced tea a Soil Conservation man came to talk about Hugh's project of turning one of the fields beyond the edge of the yard to clover for his bees. Laura remarked dreamily that there was nothing prettier than a field of crimson clover but the Soil Conservation man said Ladino or white clover produced a light honey that is more nutritious, and that seemed to settle the matter. Then he began to talk to me of the Dorseys' phenomenal production on their half-acre garden.

"A city lady," he said, "and she makes one of the finest gardens in this country."

He spoke of beans, okra, butter beans, corn, squash, beets, lettuce and potatoes. There were tomatoes that weighed two pounds. And his eyes especially brightened at the memory of raspberries and blueberries from the prickly thicket at the edge of the garden, where they started with twenty plants and harvested such an abundance of fruit that they were hard put to place it even

with their wide circle of friends and vast family connection.

"Fortunately or unfortunately, in blueberry season we seemed to have a number of friends and relatives who were in the hospital," laughed Laura. "Instead of taking them flowers we took blueberries."

So it is with all their produce. They make no attempt to preserve it for winter use but distribute it freehandedly because they feel strongly that fresh vegetables and fruits are a boon to good health and what Angelo M. Pellegrini calls "the Good Life." (I also like his quote in *The Food-Lover's Garden* from Dr. Samuel Johnson about the "enlightened company" who "mind their belly very studiously and very carefully.")

They use all natural fertilizers, lime and cottonseed meal and all the mulch they can get. The water line to their kitchen runs along the edge of the garden and they can water plants in time of drought if they happen to be there. If not, they rely on the moisture-saving mulch.

With the Dorseys gardening is hard personal work. I

suspect they have a yardman in their tree-shaded walled garden in the city with its impeccable oval of lawn and banks of evergreens and coolly fragrant white hosta lilies. But they dig and sweat and itch and scratch with the rest of us in the country and count it one of their more enduring pleasures.

Laura, who was an art major in college and returned to get her master's degree in chemistry and biology, is a student of ecology and high on organic gardening but gentle and low key in her advocacy of it.

"It's the earth I think about," she says quietly. "We have an obligation. We can't keep abusing and robbing it. We can't strip it of all that's natural and belonging and continue to live on it ourselves. I love the soil. I love to work with it and I think we should try to give back to it more than we take away."

Chapter 6

"I'm so tired. I was up all night tending my pussy willows!"

— Overheard at a flower show

EVERY WOMAN IS A FLOWER ARRANGER at heart. Increasing numbers are learning the rules and agree with Ruth Stout that "the bliss that comes from ignorance should seldom be encouraged for it is likely to do one out of a more satisfying bliss." Some, like me, are reconciled to knowing very little and are blissful blunderers of the I-know-what-I-like school. Obviously, if you think a Hogarth curve is a mountain road you're not going to be filled with misgivings at the way a wad of pansies looks in a pewter candleholder.

When I first began to see *arranged* flowers I was rendered absolutely helpless and self-conscious. My mother always had fresh flowers around the house — long-stemmed things in her grandmother's old green lemonade pitcher and short-stemmed things in various cut-glass or handpainted thingumajigs she got as wedding presents.

If she had a lot of nasturtiums she used the Christmas ambrosia bowl for them and we thought it looked good enough for church and Sunday school, where it usually ended up—on the crocheted doily with the cross worked through the middle on a table in front of the pulpit.

She didn't mention the word "arrange." She "did" the flowers and sometimes we got pretty excited about them, especially in the spring when the first ones came out. I remember a single sprig of white grancy graybeard in an old blue crock on the kitchen table that seemed so special and wonderful to us one cold gray evening in February that we just sat around the oilcloth table exulting over it, long after supper was over. Weather or no weather, spring had set foot on the land. There was the evidence.

But then I began to go to flower shows and hear the patois of arrangers and see the formidable branches of gladioli "composed" with wire and weights. I didn't understand much of anything anybody said about design, scale, balance and harmony. Rhythm and focal points and stuff like that might as well have been the language of Georgia Tech engineers. They didn't seem to have anything to do with a handful of daffodils and me. I hadn't been to Tech and besides my feet hurt.

So I returned to my raising, using wedding-present vases (usually with lumpy flowers painted on their stomachs) and sticking anything I could get my hands on into them.

It was years before I returned to a flower show and then I hit one that really got to me. It was up at the Georgia Mountain Fair. The flowers are beautiful in the mountains in August if nowhere else. There's enough rainfall and all those cool nights and they keep flourishing long after flowers have gone to seed and shriveled in lower altitudes. The Towns County Garden Club may have had another theme but as I recall the show it sort of went along with a classification dreamed up by the county agent, "Mister Nick" (E. N. Nicholson). This was called "Homemade and Handy" and Mister Nick thought it up to bring out and show off anything mountain farmers had made to use around the old homestead. Some wonderfully worn tools and household appliances with the patina of a hundred years' use on them are shown off each year. The flower show went in the same general direction, making use of many native blossoms and around-the-house containers. I forget now who arranged the "arrangement" and I'm sure it didn't win a prize but I stopped and looked at it and went back several times to admire it.

It was an old blue granite teakettle filled with Joe Pye weed. The soft mauve plumes of the roadside-creek bank wildling and its rough pointed leaves looked absolutely stunning in the battered tea kettle. Joe Pye is called "Queen of the Meadow" in the southern mountains and many of my neighbors regard it affectionately because in the old days before paved roads and easy access to doctors and drugstores they found it useful for teas and poultices. And here it was in a flower show in the homely old kettle looking beautiful and regal and special — and far more interesting than three gladioli and seven carnations or even five orchids climbing a pole, which I saw in a show once.

For some reason that teakettle of Joe Pye weed took the hex off flower arranging for me. Why shouldn't flowers be homemade and handy too? Why shouldn't you use what you have — flowers if you have them, weeds if they interest you, leaves and boughs of pine and magnolia where you can get them? When I decided that I started having fun with flowers.

A big part of the joy of flower fixing is trying to suit the container to what the arrangers call "the material." Now I think everybody, even the florists, has deserted the on-purpose vase and let his imagination have free rein. I saw an old boot with cactus growing out of a hole in the toe in Dingle, Ireland. A neighbor of mine sticks Wandering Jew and geraniums in a wooden stirrup she found in the barn. I used to keep fresh bouquets in an old ironstone chamber pot in the bathroom but I sometimes had the feeling that it was awfully darned whimsical and cute and, besides, the chamber pot leaked a little so I gave it up.

But there are containers that manage to be interesting and fun without being notional and affected. I have a few that I cherish not only because of the way they enhance whatever they hold but because of their association. Before he closed up shop to enter retirement and make way for urban renewal, Walter Bailey, who had run a hardware store on Atlanta's Decatur Street that went back to the days of wagon yards, gave me a half a peck tin measure that he used to measure out seed corn. It's a dark almost brown red and all manner of things look pretty in it but especially the first bronze chrysanthemum of the season. I couldn't be separated from a jugware vase with a broken lip that Jack picked up at a roadside junk stand once. It is uneven, obviously homemade, but its grainy brown surface has a handsome glaze and when I put sunflowers in it I feel sorry for Van Gogh, poor thing. Cream pitchers and sugar bowls are endlessly useful and adaptable and the search for new ones makes junking, especially on out-of-town trips, a continuing treasure hunt. The Salvation Army store in Miami where

Gordon Weel took me to shop yielded up a copper sugar bowl with brass handles for fifty cents—perfect for baby marigolds. A crockery cream pitcher with what the antiquers call "a line," which is to say a crack that doesn't go through, was mine for fifteen cents in a Biloxi, Mississippi, secondhand store. In the spring, cornflowers look lovely in it, picking up the uneven blue wash around its rim, and later I like to fill it with pink lilliput zinnias and spikes of blue salvia.

Baskets may be the most satisfying containers of all, particularly the old split-oak or honeysuckle ones that have been weathered and darkened by age. They seem to look their best filled with zinnias or wild flowers, masses of goldenrod, blackeyed Susans, Queen Anne's lace.

Once we stopped by a country house that was being torn down looking for building material and I wandered around the yard on the prowl for plants that might be bulldozed away. Under a spigot by the back fence was a brown ironstone vegetable dish that had been used to hold water for chickens. It had an interesting crackled, veined look and was a pretty oval shape. The owner, looking baffled at my taste, said, "Take it." I have used that old vegetable dish hundreds of times—sometimes with winter greenery, sometimes in summer for a gala assortment of daisies and red poppies. Its shallow depth is particularly suited to daffodils because they don't need any help in holding up their heads if they are firmly anchored on a needlepoint holder in enough water and the veined sepia color somehow sets off the clear gold of their blossoms. A ship captain's copper kettle, square and flat-bottomed to resist rough seas, was a Christmas gift one year that is almost in constant use, holding spring and summer bouquets equally well but really looking its best with bittersweet or some other bright-berried green.

Bottles are fine for a single bloom and a leaf and each year I find that I am growing more partial to the lone flower or the small bouquet. They accomplish that rite known as "bringing the outdoors indoors" without taking much away from the flower beds or robbing the woods. I was charmed to read somewhere that two or three violets, dug up roots and all and put in a shallow container of water with moss and rocks to anchor them, would last a lot longer than the picked bouquet and would look prettier and more natural. It's true. Every spring I get giddy at the sight of the old-fashioned gray Confederate violets which come up all over the yard, the bird's-foot violets which show their pansylike faces on dry banks along the roadside and the little white violets down by the creek bank. The children and I have brought home handfuls of them. It's hard to find something to hold them, although if you tie them together with one of those little wired tapes and put them in a small cream pitcher or a toothpick or match holder, if such survives in your household, they look pretty. Even so they wilt fast.

Now we seldom pick. We take a trowel and dig up one or two plants, preferably those with some open flowers and some buds, gently wash the dirt from their roots and arrange them in water on the pewter plate, which is one of my favorite containers. A small fern or a foam flower plant makes a congenial companion and when the children have finished adding moss and rocks from that vast collection they bring back from every walk (causing our washing machine to send out a horrendous clunking sound if you aren't careful to search blue jean pockets), the effect is woodland natural.

Late summer is the time we start collecting our dried arrangements. Really, these are collections or accumulations, rather than arrangements. I got a book on drying flowers once and had a go at storing roses and zinnias and larkspur in sifted sand and alum but I couldn't get over the idea that they came out looking slightly embalmed—if they came out at all. Let those who want to hang on to summer unnaturally long fiddle around with sand and alum, I'll ride with the season. When flowers dry, I'll take them dried—with one exception, preserved leaves. I'm mad about collecting branches from the beech tree down on the creek bank and sticking them in a mixture of glycerine and water— about one part glycerine to two parts water—until they get a soft olive green or bronze, depending upon the stage at which you cut your branches. (The light-green ones become dark green, the yellow ones become bronze.) Beech leaves are well adapted to showing off indoors and they hold their color endlessly after a glycerine-and-water soak for about four days. I retire mine when it's time for the Christmas greens, bring them out in January and finally throw them away when forced forsythia and plum branches come out of the cold downstairs bathroom closet in February.

Except for beech leaves, magnolia leaves and pine branches and the paper-white narcissus and hyacinth bulbs, which you simply have to start in pebbles and water in the fall, our winter flowers are the dried ones the children and I bring back from walks. Once, just for them, I cut the top off a plastic liquid soap container, sprayed it with dark-green paint, daubed on a little black shoe polish just to make it look faintly marbleized, and stuffed it with chicken wire. When we took walks they looked out for seed pods and ferns and interesting branches for "our 'rangement." It grew slowly over a period of months — dried dill heads, house leek and snowban blooms from the yard, mullein stalks, dock, pokeweed and various grasses from the woods. We found garlic drying in the Wolffs' pasture down the road and brought home a few flower heads — then still purplish and almost aggressively

fragrant—and added them to the pot. A branch loaded with chinaberries, which dry a soft amber color, made a focal point for our arrangement, we decided. Gradually the thing grew until we had to transfer it to a basket and when spring came I couldn't bear to throw it away but moved it to the porch where it holds the place of honor over the sink, looking a little seedy and spider-webby but still dear to us all. That sink, incidentally, is something every flower putterer needs. It's really a bar sink, bought as a bargain at a lumberyard, and it serves the double purpose of a refreshment bar and a place to water plants and arrange flowers.

The little cupboard under it holds most of my flower arranging paraphernalia and you do collect aids, even if you know next to nothing about arranging. Nobody ever had enough needlepoint holders or oasis. When you can't find the right size to fit your vase and your bouquet, it's very handy to have a swatch of chicken wire and some tin snips on hand. I've heard that you can buy swaths of chicken wire colored dark green in stores catering to flower arrangers now, but I happen to have about fifty feet of it left over from a play yard we once built to enclose the children when they were toddlers. (What a vain dream that was!)

That fine florist wire is a great help in supplying backbone to limber, bobbling flowers. You have to have it if you grow everlasting or strawflowers for winter bouquets and it's so easy to grow and so colorful you should, even if the stems and leaves give up the ghost when they begin to dry out. You can stick wires for stems into the magenta and gold and rose strawflowers, anchor them in oasis, a

wad of clay or a pot of sand, and shower them with pearly everlasting (known locally as rabbit tobacco) and you have a cheerful little nosegay for a dreary flowerless season. Blue salvia, which keeps its color and is amenable to being air dried (just tie a bunch together and hang it on the kitchen wall next to your shallots and peppers), also looks fine with strawflowers.

NOW AND THEN I am attracted by flower arranging as a precise art with rules and an ancient and honorable history. I read books and look at pictures and think I'll give it a fling someday. But women who excel at the Japanese art of flower arranging must have more perceptive families than I have.

Julia Fitch, my friend at Roswell's pretty little Arthur Smith Memorial Library, tempted me one spring day with a beautiful twenty-five-dollar book purporting to be *A Complete Guide to Japanese Ikebana.*

Technical discipline is the ticket, says Shozo Sato. None of this Western "naive, personal and on the whole haphazard" flower arranging. Leaves and rocks and flowerless branches play an important part in the Japanese method and when you have your shin (main branch) and soe (supporting branch) lined up you're on your way to being a red-hot Rikka arranger. Or so I thought.

The reason I was looking at flower-arranging books when Julia showed me this one was that I suddenly had loads of poppies, cornflowers and sweet peas and I wanted to do something absolutely smashing with them.

In vain I searched Shozo Sato's book for poppies, cornflowers and sweet peas. No soap. There are lots of gorgeous color plates and directions for bleaching broom sedge and twining thorn branches so they repeat the concave motif of the vase. You can even do wonders with silver-colored wire mesh, using no flowers at all, or dazzle your friends with three eucalyptus branches and five anemones. If you move to the informal section you can spray some birch branches with white paint and create "a sense of windswept motion" with those and five daffodils. Only I didn't have any daffodils left at that season and no time to mess around painting sticks when I hadn't even got my nasturtiums planted.

But the simplicity of the Japanese arrangement is certainly appealing and I decided to leave my poppies, cornflowers and sweet peas where they were and do something fetching with a single rose, a hosta leaf and a corky branch from the sweetgum tree.

My son was the first to notice.

"What are you doing on the mantel?" he asked.

"Not doing," I said pertly. "It's done. A Japanese flower arrangement."

He looked again.

"Do you like it?" I asked anxiously. "Do you think it would be better if I let the water show and maybe put in a rock?"

"Hm-m-n," he said and put a record on the record player.

"Well, don't you like it?" I persisted. "The Japanese are so much better at these things than we are. Every single detail is fraught with . . . er imagery and symbolism.

"Remember Pearl Harbor," he said and left the room.

My daughter came and noted that I was using a vase instead of the baskets and old pitchers that I had been addicted to in my pre-shin-soe-and-tai-saki days.

"It's not very _flowery_ looking, is it?" she asked.

"I should say not," I said. "Line and texture and feeling are there. Not flowers. Do you sense the somber mood . . . ?

"Of that stick?" she asked. "Yes, ma'am."

To prove to her that I was on to something great I made her wash her hands and look at the gorgeous twenty-five-dollar library book. She said it was spectacular and I was right to learn all about the technique in case I have time for a hobby in my old age. She even admitted a color plate featuring worm-eaten wood and three irises was pretty stylish looking.

"But I still like flowers," she said. "Why grow 'em if you don't use 'em?"

"Banal," I said. "Absolutely stinkingly banal."

And then I went out and apologized to my poppies, cornflowers and sweet peas. Helter-skelter, haphazard and unarranged, they were the prettiest things I ever saw.

Chapter 7

"There's not a sprig of grass that shoots uninteresting to me."

—Thomas Jefferson at the age of forty-three

"I'm still devoted to the garden... Although an old man I am but a young gardener."

—Mr. Jefferson twenty-five years later

OF ALL THE THINGS WRITTEN by Thomas Jefferson, including—I blush to admit—the Declaration of Independence, the only one that has ever kept me in a state of delinquency at the public library is his *Garden Book*. How I love that *Garden Book*!

For years I thought it was out of print and I kept the library's copy out shamefully long, hoping the computer would forget who had it, the way I sometimes forget when I lend a book. Naturally, it did not.

Under penalty of returning and paying up or losing my indispensable library card, I would relinquish Mr. Jefferson, only to edge back into the stacks and check him out again when no body was looking. Finally, Jim and Florence Corley, neighbors twenty miles away, visited Monticello and found the American Philosophical Society of Philadelphia had brought the book out again. They bought me a copy and I have improved many a winter night since reading and rereading it.

It's not that Mr. Jefferson's garden prose sings. It does and it doesn't. He bolsters and affirms all gardening with statements like this:

"I have often thought that if heaven had given me my choice of position and calling, it should have been on a rich spot of earth, well watered, and near a good market for the productions of the garden. No occupation is so delightful to me as the culture of the earth, and no culture comparable to that of the garden."

Or this: "Those who labour in the earth are the chosen people of God, if ever he had a chosen people, whose breasts he has made his peculiar deposit for substantial and genuine virtue."

But, of course, not every reader's pulse will hammer at page-long discussions of the Hessian fly or the interminable lists of things Mr. Jefferson has planted or wants planted. Mine do. When I read that on March 10, 1779, he "bought another Aegyptian Acacia from Greenspring. It is in blossom," I feel a tremendous kinship with this founding father.

When I read, "April 29, 1804. Planted seeds of the Cherokee rose from Gov. Milledge (of Georgia) in a row of about 6 f. near the NE corner of the Nursery," I can't wait to turn the pages until I find if that rose flourished. *Seeds*, yet!

Mr. Jefferson loved the weather. Not many days passed that he didn't write down what it was doing. When he writes "Great fresh in the Rivanna this day," I am excited, although I have never seen the Rivanna and am not sure what one of its "freshes" amounts to.

But the really inspiring thing about Mr. Jefferson as a gardener is that he kept, really kept, gardening records. He started his journal in 1766, _before_ the Declaration of Independence, mind you, and with comparatively few lapses kept it up until the autumn of 1824, two years before his death. That's fifty-eight years of faithfully setting down his aspirations and achievements in his particular "labour in the earth."

Everybody tells you to keep such a record. It's very helpful, they say, to note the dates when you planted seeds and bulbs and the weather conditions. You not only won't be mystified when funny-looking little things start coming up where you forgot planting anything, you'll know exactly how long it took for those seeds to germinate and whether rain or sun or an unseasonable cool spell helped things along.

The most common excuse I have heard — and offered — for not keeping records is that there simply isn't time enough to work in a garden and to write about it. You have to choose one or the other.

Mr. Jefferson had conflicts. He served as Minister Plenipotentiary to France from 1784 to 1789. He served as Secretary of State in George Washington's cabinet and, of course, put in a stint as President of the United States for the two terms beginning in 1800. This meant traveling far from his beloved Monticello and keeping track of things by slow and erratic mail. It meant spending money he wanted for plants and seeds on other things. (My heart ached for this President of the United States when he wrote from Washington in 1807: "I had hoped to keep the expenses of my office within the limits of its salary, so as to apply my private income entirely to the improvement and enlargement of my estate; but I have not been able to do it.")

Even gardeners with lesser jobs and estates will recognize that pinch — the old conflict between a loaf of bread and a hyacinth, the stomach and the soul.

But Mr. Jefferson persevered with his gardening and with his reports on it. What he failed to set down in the ledger, which he had designated for his gardening records, he wrote somewhere — on a random scrap of paper or in a letter to a friend. His letters to workers back home are almost all filled with directions for planting. His correspondence with personal friends runs heavily to reports on seeds and soil, experiments with plants and notice that he is sending them something.

Typical is this letter to a woman friend in France: "On the 26th October 1805 I had the pleasure of writing to you and informing you that I then made up for you a box of seeds acorns and nuts, which were to go by a vessel from Baltimore to Nantes ... "

The fact that Mr. Jefferson, whose responsibilities somewhat exceeded mine, could find time to keep a garden book has on occasion pushed me into keeping a sort of journal and I strongly recommend it. The first one was a small five-cent notebook that would fit into my blue jeans pocket. We had not moved to the country then but worked a small garden spot by Jack's creek bank on weekends. I noted in my book every day that we came to the country and what we did. It might be one line: "Planted pole beans." Or, "Beans up."

Slight record that it was, the next year when I took it out and reread it I found it as engrossing as _War and Peace_. One penciled line evoked for me the day, the color of the sky, the texture of the earth and the feel of the sun on my back when I leaned over to press a seed into the soil.

The next journal I tried was considerably more ambitious. I had moved to the country by this time and my contact with gardening projects was pretty daily. I attempted to write something every day, winter and summer, about the state of the earth and what, if anything, I was doing about it. Like Mr. Jefferson, I was fascinated by the weather and observed it closely, setting down its vagaries in detail.

Naturally this journal flourished for a few weeks and fizzled out. I really didn't have time to carry on to that extent. I finally resorted to the method employed by country women since the beginning of time when they put a hen to set. I scribbled on the kitchen calendar a word or two to tell me when I got the okra seeds or the beets in the ground.

That, I might say, is a useful record and better than none at all. But record keeping can be a great gardening aid and tremendous fun, depending upon how you do it and how much time and effort you have to devote to it.

Herbert Tabor, a mountain friend who had the pret-

tiest gardens in the world when he was a bit younger and
strong, kept simple records. He had little tabs that he
stuck first in the cold frame by the basement window,
where he started his tomatoes and then in the ground
when he transplanted them. On these he noted the variety he planted and the date. For pure pleasure he aug-
mented this record with photographs, taken at intervals
during the season to show the progress. Not many gardeners I know have his kind of progress to report —
spinach theatrically climbing an the way to the second
story of his big old-fashioned house, making a dark-green
screen against the moming sun, squash that cross the
creek at the edge of his garden and climb the hill beyond,
cucumbers that cover trellises, and beans that look like
yard-long emerald fringe. His photographic slides are
spectacular and it's very pleasant on a winter evening
when the snow is on the North Georgia hills to pull up to
the oil burner in the Tabor living room in Ellijay and
relive the warm and beneficent days of summer by looking once again at his corn tassels dipping and bobbing in
the breeze, framed by dahlias as big as soup plates.

One gardener I know combines a written diary with
pictures. When she first clears away the winter mulch in
early spring and applies those standbys — one sack of
lime, one sack of cottonseed meal, one sack of cow
manure — she writes down the state of the soil, what was
done to it and takes a picture. As the season progresses
she continues this dual record, pasting the pictures,
which she takes with a cheap and easy camera, into the
book alongside the written word. Her garden journals are
fun principally because they reveal as much about her
development as a photographer as her growing gardening

skills. The first pictures are flat and pretty pedestrian, the standard shots showing a stark piece of earth with some scrabbly-looking weeds on it and a wheelbarrow nearby holding sacks of soon-to-be-applied nutrients. A bit later there'll be a shot of a child knee deep in radishes or a man's hand holding a rather impressive tomato. But the last of her garden journals that I saw disclosed a growing talent as a botanical photographer. She has acquired the patience and the artistry to photograph flowers and fruit up close, and the results are lovely.

The best of all garden journals, I believe, is the planning book. Mr. Jefferson did a lot of this and along about mid-July I wish that I had done the same. That is the season when the what-might-have-been's get you. It's too late to plant many of the things that you really meant to get into the ground last spring. Maddeningly enough, you can't even remember what many of them were.

For some time I have played around with a dream of making the terrace, where we gather in the late afternoons or cook out on the weekends, a little oasis in the midst of green foliage and white blossoms. It is shaded from the hot western sun by the house and screened from the road by what we grandly call "the east wing." This palatial-sounding addition is from two log cabins that I acquired, tore down, moved and combined to make another bedroom and bath and a loft room for visiting grandchildren. As that structure went up, attached to the original cabin by a breezeway, I realized that I would no longer need the trellis, which we built originally to screen us from the road, nor the bank of forsythia beyond it. The new log walls would also shelter the terrace from the north wind, leaving it exposed only to the east and the south. It offered all sorts of possibilities for the cool green and white garden I wanted.

One bitter windy evening in February, Laura Dorsey and I inspected the terrace by flashlight and I told her of my dream. I would move the viburnum carlcephalum from the chimney corner and the forsythia and Carolina jessamine and replace them with things that grew low and bloomed white and fragrant. But what? Ferns and mint, Laura said, and maybe some of the elegant white hostas. But what else? We talked of gardenias but I can't remember if she advised for or against them.

So far I have only partially realized my green and white dream. Lilies of the valley bloom under the old peach trees in the spring and I do have one bed by the kitchen wall where mint and wild fern fight for dominance. I set pots of tuberous begonias under the peach trees when the season for lilies of the valley passes and they flourish, except for one minor detail. The handsomest plant is turning out pink, not white. I have two nicotiana plants and one shasta daisy (I meant to have more) and a keg and a barrel and a strawberry jar planted with white sultana.

The kitchen window box, which is very much in evidence from the terrace, got its usual spring planting of white petunias and red geraniums, mostly because I couldn't think of anything else to stick in there. Now that it's too late for such decision making I can think of numbers of things — ferns and more white sultanas, among them.

But that shows you the wisdom of a garden-planning book. If I had been methodical in my dreaming I would have pasted the pictures and clippings that gave me the idea in the first place into a loose-leaf notebook. And somewhere in there I would have set down a plant list and the name of the nursery specializing in such material. This would have been easy to do on those February evenings when my bedtime reading runs heavily to seed catalogues.

There are many fine and informative garden books and our newspapers abound in advice from the experts. The trouble is finding the word when you are in a hurry, with planting time breathing down your neck and fifteen minutes to get half a dozen little seedlings stuck in somewhere before you have to dash for an appointment. I don't recommend that you take a course in librarianship (more properly called library science, I believe) and index every single garden book and periodical in your possession. But if you know what you're likely to need when you encounter it in your reading, it's a joy to find that you made a note of it in your journal.

It happened that I noted Angelo Pellegrini's lyrical

discussion of shallots when I read _The Food-Lovers Garden_ and was able to find it with a minimum of effort when the start of little brown bulbs Laura gave me began to multiply by the garden walk.

This may not be real efficiency but for some of us anything is profitable if it helps us squeeze a minute extra out of a crowded day to spend in the garden.

As Mr. Jefferson wrote President Washington in 1792, trying to beg off serving as Secretary of State:

"I have, therefore, no motive to consult but my own inclination, which is bent irresistibly on the tranquil enjoyment of my family, my farm, and my books."

Chapter 8

"According to the record of the rocks, insects preceeded man on this planet by quite some time, and pessimists contend that they will be the last to leave it."

—Ralph B. Swain

THERE'S A THEORY circulating among my friends and neighbors that I don't rise up and do battle against the creeping, crawling, hopping, flying, boring, sucking wild life that makes free with my garden because I'm either too lazy or too squeamish.

And while there's an element of truth in this theory, it's not the whole truth. The whole truth is that I'm too ignorant and too scared. I don't know enough about insect life to dare to tamper with it . . . much.

My friend Mrs. Ralph Sauls, a lady now in her seventies, once told me a story out of her own childhood that made a big impression on me. She said she was visiting an aunt who raised chickens and for the first time saw the miracle of an egg hatching. Somebody had explained to her that the little pecking sound she heard within an egg was a baby chicken trying to make his way out into the world.

To the gentle little girl the shell seemed to be a prison and when nobody was around she decided to help the tiny prisoners escape. She cracked and pulled away egg shells and all the little chickens died from premature freedom — exposure.

Overwhelmed by shock and grief she held out sticky little hands to her aunt and cried inconsolably. Her cry was the cry of benevolent meddlers the world over: "I was just trying to *help*!"

Her aunt comforted her and then gave her a piece of stern advice all of us need at times.

"Alberta," she said, "always remember this: *Keep your hands off what you don't understand!*"

I don't understand garden pests.

The last United States Department of Agriculture tome I saw on the subject estimated that there may be as many as 1,500,000 different kinds of insects in the world and the injurious species in the United States could run between 6500 and 10,000.

The catch is that some of these are harmful in one stage and beneficial in another, and it takes time to wait around and see if a leaf-gnawing worm may grow up, go legit and earn his keep by becoming an aphid-eating beetle. The suspense is debilitating and all that getting up at night and running through the garden with the flashlight to see what is happening under the tomato leaves and in the innermost heart of the cabbage certainly takes its toll of the next day's work.

But it does seem to me that we have an obligation to know what we're doing, whom we are killing, when we grab up a bottle of spray or a packet of lethal dust. It's perfectly obvious that without insect life on earth things would come to a pretty pass. There might not be any vegetation at all. And although I don't for a minute imagine that my ninety-eight-cent can of poison spray will annihilate a whole species of insect and thereby throw what the ecologists call "the totality of interrelationships" out of kilter, I do worry that I might kill villains and heroes indiscriminately, repay the kindness of my invaluable friends, the birds, with a case of acute gastritis and possibly even jeopardize the health and well-being of those great gardening assistants, my grandchildren.

If I had vast acreage at stake I might feel differently. In fact I might make so much money off my broad airplane-dusted fields that I could afford to haul my family and friends off to some pollution-free spot (if there is any left) to wait until the poison cloud settled. But in my little patch if the eggplant turns to lace-and-drawn work — and it does — I just take eggplant off the menu and

when I have dinner guests I let 'em eat squash. (This is a terrible deprivation, too, because thanks to Julia Fitch and Ben Pace, a peerless vegetable grower and eater, I have two eggplant recipes that turn that bland vegetable into something sumptuous.)

When one of my red rose buds, whose unfolding I await with great excitement, doesn't unfold at all but looks like it was scorched with a hot iron I'm not exactly serene and accepting. I stomp around looking for the culprit and swearing vengeance. And when great ripening tomatoes, just hours from the table, come down with cancerous sores, the sound of my weeping, wailing and gnashing of teeth rends the country quiet.

Nevertheless, before I launch chemical warfare I feel compelled to know more about what I am doing. The experts, although saving us from plagues of locusts and boll weevil and potato famines in the past, have had their moments of doubt and error. Remember how jubilant we all were about the way DDT disposed of flies and other household pests? (In South Alabama I know old-timers who still sing hosannas to it for giving us a generation or two of freedom from bedbugs alone.) The trouble was that the few pests that escaped the spray fled to bosky dells somewhere where they regrouped and promptly produced DDT-resistant offspring. So it looks like the only recourse is bigger and more deadly sprays. To be followed by bigger and more resistant pests? It's a grim prospect.

There must be a better way and I believe it begins with studying insects well enough to be able to identify them. The handiest book I have for this is Ralph B. Swain's *The Insect Guide: Orders and Major Families of North American Insects.* The pictures really look like the insects I encounter in life and the text is easy, concise and oddly enjoyable. In addition to telling you which of your crops the chewer or sucker is likely to attack, it adds nice little gossipy notes about the minute monster's home life. For instance, Bessybugs. They are members of the prominent Passalidae family and, it occurred to me, probably in the South called Betsybug, which your relatives frequently say, "You haven't any more sense than." These citizens live under rotten logs and "bestow great care upon the young," even chewing the wood before their babies eat it. And the larvae of carpet beetles, officially _Derméstes maculàtus_, are sometimes used by museum workers "to clear the dried flesh from the delicate skeletons of small animals."

In fact, if this book has a fault it's that when you tear into the house sweating and breathing fire to look up some strange bug you might get so absorbed in reading about why the scarab was sacred in Egypt or how fireflies

use their lights as a signal for mating that you forget entirely about the Critter waiting in the jelly glass for identification.

Once you have identified the bug—and a magnifying glass is good for this—and know what to expect of it, if it prefers cabbage to carrots, for instance (and most insects eat one kind of plant, ignoring other kinds), then you can decide for yourself how far you want to go in poisoning him and his relatives and, incidentally, some of the air and the earth.

To me there are other routes that are appealing because they seem less drastic, more imaginative and just plain interesting.

My neighbors Jerry and Polly Eaves, notable for building the settlement's first swimming pool, are also impressive because—they leave insect control to a family of potracking guineas.

Guineas never touch a vegetable or a flower, they tell me, because they sate themselves on juicy bugs. Even better, they make such an infernal racket that the young Eaveses practically never see a snake. Snakes, being lovers of peace and quiet, take to the tall timber to avoid the clatter of guineas.

For some time I've thought of installing a few guineas at Sweet Apple, but recently bantam chickens have taken my eye. They are peerless when it comes to insect pests, my neighbors tell me, amazingly prolific and hardly ever touch garden truck unless a low-growing and flamboyant tomato takes their eye. The care needed by domestic fowls has deterred me so far, but my neighbor Olivia Johnson says she will give me a start of banties—a rooster and two hens—out of her very next setting of eggs. And I'll take them, I think, because my mother says a country place doesn't seem furnished if you don't have at least one rooster to crow and a few hens to supply eggs for the table and fertilizer for the garden.

Somewhere I read that turkeys are highly recommended as garden police and if they eat their weight in bugs, as birds are said to do, it would be an orgy to end all orgies. Ducks and geese have been used in some places to eat the insects and weed strawberry beds and cotton fields. Generally they have a reputation for sticking to business and leaving garden crops alone, but I've heard that ducks have a secret yen for young onions, especially in the spring, and since I only plant one row of onions, one row of shallots and a small bed of chives it wouldn't take a duck on a spree long to decimate my entire crop. Funny, while ducks relish young onions, rabbits, they tell me, abhor them and won't even darken the garden that is surrounded with onions.

Enlisting the aid of fowls to handle weed and pest control appeals as a simple and direct approach. So is hand-picking the bugs from the plant and dropping them in a bucket of kerosene but ah, how I hate that job, particularly those big soft green horned cutworms. It seems easier to make paper-cup or foil collars for the tomato plants when they are young and it works. I've noticed that if you can get a young tomato plant up some size it doesn't seem attractive to cutworms. Other things move in, of course, but there's a saying among organic gardeners that if the soil is good and the plant is strong and healthy it will probably survive, and I believe it. The idea is maximum biological efficiency in your department to throw off the effect of insect attackers, as human beings in the pink frustrate disease germs.

Gardening lore is full of all kinds of safe home remedies for pest control, some of them time tested and some of them, I suspect, old wives' tales. Since I am in the midst of trying some of them for the first time I can't vouch for their effectiveness. I can say they add a new element of excitement to gardening.

There are hideous brews, of course, which I won't try except as a desperate, last-ditch measure — urine to repel grasshoppers, for instance, and an evil potion made by picking off the most troublesome bugs, putting them in a bottle containing a little water and letting them decompose. The resulting juice is said to be very efficacious as a spray because most insects have a superstitious way of avoiding the dead bodies of their own kind. You try it if you like, but I lost my license to practice witchcraft.

My sage, which Olivia planted for me back of the woodpile one spring day when I thought it was too hot for the young plants to survive, flourishes on neglect. But watch it, warns another neighbor, there are certain people whose very touch will kill sage. These include menstruating women.

The nicest and most interesting garden health measures are plant repellents or the practice of companionate planting. Janet Gillespie advanced the cause of marigolds in her book, *Peacock Manure and Marigolds*. This smelly little beauty affects some insects as it does some people. They turn up their sensitive noses and move out of its range. Its roots are also said to excrete something which kills soil nematodes. So I edge my garden with dwarf marigolds and plant the tall beauties anywhere I can find a spot to stick them. They have blossoms almost as big as football-season chrysanthemums and one package of seed, started early in a flat in the house, goes further than practically anything you can buy.

Garlic is also said to be as effective in holding some insects at arm's length as it does some people. I planted a bulb beside each rosebush, and next year I'm hoping to have enough to stick them around every peach tree to see if they will turn back the borers.

Up at Chadwick's, the old-time general store which has served the people of this area for more than a hundred years, when you buy your turnip and mustard seeds loose from the big seed bins, instead of in the more expensive packages with pictures on them, they will throw in a scoop of radish seed. It's the custom of the country to sow them all together, counting on the radishes to save the mustard and turnips from lice. So far I have a good stand of young greens without a sign of trouble anywhere. Radishes are also said to protect squashes from squash bugs.

The stinging nettle school interested me. This powerful plant (advocated as an aphrodisiac in old herbals) is said by old gardeners to repel aphids and to enrich the soil. So I left a few plants in my salad-green bed expecting great results. Olivia is so kindhearted she hated to tell me that those stalwart nettles I was counting on weren't stinging nettles at all but another kind of scratchy weed which was not only of no value but could become a pest itself.

Anything that is strong-smelling seems to excite or disgust bugs. Even a fragrant hand lotion will draw so

many bees, yellow jackets and gnats on a summer morning that you have to come in the house and wash with yellow soap. The herb fragrances which are a delight to people — mint, rosemary and sage — are said to disgust the cabbage buttery. Corn borers, according to some observers, can't work within range of geranium or marigold smell. Santolina and southernwood, which I have planted on the rock wall near the porch, should by all accounts be in the garden to keep away moths. And let's see, there are moth balls which will keep away rabbits if scattered around the lettuce patch and black pepper which, if sprinkled around squash vines, will repel squash borers. (An old recipe for keeping houseflies, blowflies and those nasty green bottle flies away from the gardener is to wash your clothes in soap suds to which oil of anise has been added.)

Just as there are plants that jog along together happily neighboring, there are many others that seem to offend each other. Tomatoes are good neighbors to asparagus, they say, repelling the asparagus beetle, but poor neighbors to peppers and corn, drawing the same kind of pests.

Wood ashes, which I have in abundant supply in fireplace weather, go on my garden automatically and I don't have any way of knowing if they turn back hordes of maggot flies and scab, as they are supposed to do. I put them there because of the somewhat vague assurance of most of my gardening friends that they are "good for the soil." Since I haven't seen any maggot flies or beetle scab I like to believe it's true. It may be that maggot flies and scab didn't see anything that interested them in my small patch and passed on to better pickings.

Anyhow, I have to put the ashes somewhere and I like the idea that they are working in the garden. The same is true of mint. After years of being unable to grow mint I suddenly found myself going down for the third time in oceans of spearmint, lemon, pineapple and peppermint, not to mention their cousin, catnip. I started pulling it out of flower beds with a heavy hand and hauling it to the raw clay bank across the road where I'm trying to get something—anything—to grow.

"You know, they say snakes won't go around mint," Laura Dorsey remarked casually.

"They *won't?*" I cried.

Being of a scientific bent, Laura wasn't about to give me any gold-plated guarantee but she did tell me this story. When they first settled their old house on the hill in Cherokee County they kept finding snake skins on the fireboard in the living room and this struck cold terror to the hearts of the young girls in the family, as it would to mine if I knew a snake was sneaking into my house unbeknownst to me to make his seasonal change of clothes.

"I planted mint around all the foundations and by the steps and the snake skins didn't appear again," Laura related.

However, the snake himself showed up in the tool house. He was harmless, a kind of pest repellent in fact, but he also repelled Laura so she planted mint around the tool house. She never saw the snake there again.

"Where did he go, I wonder?" I mused, thinking of distant mintless regions.

"To the privy," said Laura. "I'm planting mint around it now."

I'm planting mint, too, everywhere there's an untenanted inch of ground and in some places where I have to pull up other things.

Chapter 9

"Some men go into the wilderness to slay... Others—
the gentle hunters—go armed with basket and trowel,
for the quarry they would track are green growing
things that they hope to keep alive..."

— Richardson Wight

MY MOTHER ONCE KNEW an old country woman whose age
and state of decrepitude so fretted her grandchildren that
they arrived one day and persuaded her to close up her
house and go to the City to live with them.

A week later Muv saw Granny Helton back in her
own yard hoeing her onions. She couldn't help remarking
that the old lady's sojourn in the city had been a short
one.

"I don't say a word agin Sis and her crew," Granny
said loyally. "Them's good young'uns and they treated me
fine as snuff. I shore had me a high-heel time there in
town."

"Well, you didn't stay long," Muv noted.

Granny put down her hoe and drew closer, within whispering distance.

"I ain't a-telling everybody this," she confided, "but would you believe that Sis ain't got a feather bed in her house? *Entersprings*, good woman, *entersprings* on every bedstead! It's more than human flesh can endure!"

Muv started to say a word in defense of that modern innovation, innerspring mattresses, but the old lady interrupted with more shocking revelations on the poor pass to which her beloved granddaughter had come.

"*Eggs*!" she whispered fiercely. "Sis ain't got a hen on the place! Nor a rooster to crow for day. That pore young'un sends to the store for every bite of rations they put in their mouth! Even *eggs*!"

Muv had to sympathize with her there. Poor Sis had indeed hit bottom. But Sis and her "crew" didn't think so and the next week they were back to get Granny and her house plunder and take her off for another go at city living. This time they sold most of Granny's furniture, gave away her quilts and crocheted doilies and loaded her winter and summer clothes into the back of their station wagon. Muv was comforted to notice, as they passed her house, that Granny's feather bed and a coop of chickens had been secured to the roof of the station wagon with a length of clothesline.

Nevertheless, in a month or two Granny caught a bus from the city, unbeknownst to Sis, and came back to her cold, unfurnished, closed-up house. The neighbors thought they saw lights and the next day when they investigated they found she had spread herself a pallet in front of the fireplace with the one ragged old quilt left on the place and died there during the night.

EVERY TIME I TRY to make myself a wild-flower garden I think of Granny Helton.

Not every wildling suffers the way Granny did at being uprooted but so many of them do, it behooves all of us who love them to be very, very careful.

Wild-flower gardens have become mighty popular in recent years. Garden clubs and other groups interested in ecology and preservation of natural areas have started all of us to thinking about native plants. Shopping centers, suburban housing developments, apartment complexes and superhighways are rapidly gobbling up the open lands and remaining forests. The voices of the power saw and bulldozer are heard in the land.

It's natural that people who told time by dandelions, forecast their love life with daisies and gathered maypops as children can't bear to think of the time when their children and grandchildren will not see wild flowers outside of greenhouses and preserves. The compulsion to get there with trowel and shovel ahead of the destroyers is strong in a lot of us.

When I first moved to Sweet Apple I thought a wild-flower garden would be a snap. With five mostly wooded acres to work on, it would be just a matter of encouraging what was there and judiciously augmenting the existing wild-flower population with choice additions mooched from other landowners or snatched from the path of bulldozers.

The only equipment I had for the task was a love of wild flowers and that dangerous thing—a little, very little, knowledge.

As a child in South Alabama I had roamed the pinewoods afoot and by horseback and had covered all the navigable streams in our area by a sort of flat-bottomed canoe or pirogue, which we called a double-ender. I always came home with a scraggly bouquet of something or hands full of leaves, which my mother or some of the women in the quarters would identify for me.

Liz-Beth, a Cajun woman shunned by blacks and whites alike as a "no-nation woman" because of her mixed French, Indian and Negro ancestry, turned out to be the most knowledgeable of all about plants. Coot, our cook, suggested darkly that she was a "conjur woman" and it was true that she knew a lot of magicky things about plants. Holly trees repel evil spirits, fern seeds make you invisible, deer tongue leaves placed in the quilt shelf make the bedding smell sweet and sweet basil worn in your shoe will guarantee that you'll see your true love before moonup. But her great charm for me was that she loved to walk in the woods and see things and greet every blossom, every bush, every tree with the eyes of an old friend who knew its name. At least she knew one name for everything. I often wish that she had known the botanical names because I may have learned them then. I haven't been able to since.

Liz-Beth early convinced me that what Jean Hersey says about identifying plants is true. When you learn a stranger's name, where he lives and something about him, you feel you have made a new friend.

"Similarly," Jean Hersey adds, "you establish rapport with an unfamiliar flower when you learn its name, something about how it grows, and where it comes from. When you meet this flower again, in another location, it fairly leaps to greet you."

So I came to Sweet Apple confident that I would be among friends in the woods, being on a name-knowing basis with a lot of plants. The only trouble was that there's a big difference between what grows in the swamps and along the beaches of South Alabama and what grows in the foothills of the North Georgia mountains. I recognized some things but failed to recognize so many that I started traveling with a wild-flower book beside me when I rode through the country or even down the road in the pick-up truck to dump the garbage. (Jean Hersey's *Wildflowers to Know and Grow* is a handy portable size and has conveniently arranged color pictures of most of the flowers in my area.)

The trouble begins, of course, when you acquire a bowing acquaintance. It's like a second-time encounter with a charmer at a bus stop. One thing leads to another and pretty soon you're wanting to take Bouncing Bet or Joe Pye home with you.

Many of these plants, like Granny Helton, didn't want to be moved. But if they do go they want their own feather beds in which to rest their bones and home-grown, humusy soil, not store-bought chemical food to nurture them. Even then they may not make it.

And one of the big problems is always when you get them where will you put them?

Garden writers who will draw you scale patterns for

planting perennials and annuals with little scallops neatly labeled here for phlox or there for lobelia, are strangely reticent about where to plant wild flowers. They say if you have a creek or a brook or maybe a little pond... I don't. That handsome outcropping of rock now... My land was planted to cotton in the old days and all the rocks of impressive dimensions must have been hauled away.

They're big on woodland paths and naturalizing things. But a path needs a destination and the children's tree house, which I can see from the back yard, somehow didn't seem the thing. They've hauled so much junk up from the dump to furnish it that I try not to look, much less walk, that way. I can't visualize mayapples and trilliums lighting the way to the sawdust pile either.

Sticking a wild plant here or there among what we country people call the "tame" flowers was certainly not recommended by anybody. I did have a patch of grass

down the hill that ran heavily to oxeye daisies—and there's always the picture of a field of daisies in full bloom in every wild-flower book. But daisies don't last forever and the time before they bloom and the time after they bloom both seem interminable. Dock and briars and wild mustard move in and I usually end up mowing it.

So I puttered with wild flowers and accomplished nothing for a time. Ferns are easy to transplant and I've had a lot of pleasure from those I planted in my green garden by the terrace. Their roots are shallow and if you get a fair amount of woods earth with them and keep them watered in hot weather they will flourish all summer, die down if there's a very hard winter freeze, and return again with the spring.

Foam flower is a charming little creek bank habitue with slender spikes of white flowers and pointed leaves that turn bronze in the fall. It likes the cool and shady

spot beneath the terrace spigot and beside the dogs' water pan.

There's a bare and sunny spot between the rail fence and the road and I have tried butterfly weed, the beautiful Turk's cap lily, which grows splendidly in the fence row down the road, and even blackeyed Susans there. The lily and the butterfly weed were quick to die. The black-eyed Susans took a little longer but die they did, after I had brought as much dirt as I could carry with them and mulched and watered them faithfully. It was pretty irritating to see that gorgeous convocation of black-eyed Susans popping up in a weedy space in Jack's field, where he sowed pasture grass a couple of years ago. They grow there by the hundreds with peasant, picture-book faces and sturdy stems that make them stand up well when you pick them for a basket bouquet. No mulch, no water—just a worn-out field with heavy clay that cracks in the heat.

The answer, I've decided, is seeds. Most wild things resist being dug up and moved. But if you will collect their seeds in the fall and scatter them in a congenial spot I believe they will spring up with alacrity and go on from there. The spot doesn't even have to be particularly congenial.

There's that mullein by the back door. Mullein (more formally, _Verbascum thapsus)_ is a handsome plant, beginning with a rosette of gray-white woolly leaves and usually peaking out six or seven feet skyward in a noble spike of yellow flowers. My neighbor Duka Wolff dug up a small one and brought it indoors in a pot a couple of years ago and it made an unusual and interesting house plant. I thought to put one in a border somewhere after the manner of Mrs. Lillian Plunkett, who gardens in Biloxi, Mississippi. Mrs. Plunkett, widow of a physician, takes an interest in the medicinal properties of most plants. But it's not mullein's much vaunted use for infusions or as a demulcent that causes her to faithfully retain a few plants in her flower border each year. She has a sentimental attachment for mullein because it grew in her mother's garden.

So I transplanted mulleins, which fortunately are in bountiful supply in my neighborhood, because they died as fast as I moved them. One spring day, to my astonishment, a mullein I *didn't* plant appeared between the bricks of the terrace by the back door. It was in the way — just where the screen door would hit it every time I went in and out, and I suspected that it was crowding the white tulips I had planted in a nearby bed. It may have, at that, because the tulips didn't show last spring but the mullein is now two years old and has a pair of flower-topped stalks, the senior of which is eight feet tall. I couldn't bear to move it and I'm glad because it is the most magnificent mullein I ever saw.

Happy as I am with that mullein, it doesn't seem hospitable to question how it got there. But the handiest explanation is that when the children and I threw out one of our dried "'rangements" we spilled some of the seeds from the brown and stiff mullein spike on the bricks of the terrace.

Almost any wild flower can be propagated by seeds, I think. The wild azalea, called by William Bartram "the most gay and brilliant flowering shrub yet known," has always been ticklish to move, even by such experts as Fred Galle, director of horticulture at Callaway Gardens, where they specialize in wild azaleas on their famous Wildflower Trail. They do move them, of course, severely root-pruning them and nursing them along a couple of years before transplanting them to a spot in the woods where they are to stay. Mr. Galle thinks layering is a "more satisfactory" way of propagating this plant, but best of all to get a large number of plants is to collect the seeds in the fall and grow your own. The seedlings are variable and may not have the same brilliant color as their parent, Mr. Galle warns, but they will come close — and azaleas, bless them, range in color from white to pale pink to deep rose and yellow and orange and are enchantingly fragrant. Mr. Galle collects seeds from the brown capsules in the fall just as they are beginning to brown up and before they open. The seeds are very fine and he stores the capsules until they are dry and shakes or cracks them to extract all the tiny seeds, which average about two hundred to the pod. These are sown on ground sphagnum moss, which has been moistened and pressed into a pot or a flat and watered in. Germination begins within thirty days, but don't look for flowers for four or five years. Sometimes it takes eight or ten years.

Two friends of mine, Andrew Sparks and Leonard Foote, lucked into some choice wild azalea seeds from a fantastically beautiful and fairly rare mountain plant and are growing them in peat pots under lights in their basements. The last I heard their plants were only an inch or so high.

That's interesting work and I hope to try it myself one day but it's too slow for the woodland trail I have in mind. Lacking a destination for a meandering walk through the woods, I decided to change the driveway from a straight shot from the road up beside the house. For one thing, that straight driveway was ugly, there wasn't turn-around room and there were always cars parked in it, reflecting the sun's rays on every surface and spoiling the view of trees and sky. It occurred to me one day that if we started the driveway down the road a bit and let it wander up to the back of the house we would have a vastly more interesting entrance. The cars wouldn't be so blatantly obvious from either the road or the cabin windows. My daughter Mary and two or three of the children were here and we sat under the apple tree in our house-coats one morning, drinking coffee and talking about it. Ruben Nunley, a neighbor who has a big earth-moving tractor and had been doing some basement excavation for me, dropped by and I mentioned the new driveway to him.

"Let's walk over it and see what you have in mind," he suggested.

So we all plunged into the woods, trampling down poison ivy, fighting brambles and climbing over stumps and decaying logs.

That night when I arrived from town there was my new driveway, a little one-lane road winding up a slight hill through pines and poplars and, of course, poison ivy. It was by no means finished but it was easy to see that on either side of the road I would have perfect filtered shade for naturalizing clumps of ferns, wild azaleas, sweet shrub and maybe blue flags and violets.

It isn't planted yet. We have been too busy hauling visitors' cars out of the mud, bringing in crushed rock and installing culverts. When winter comes again and I no longer have to worry about these things and snakes I hope to clear out the underbrush and rotting logs and start planting a few wildings. In preparation we started some things — a crab apple tree, wild azaleas and sweet shrub — in sand and peat moss back in the shade of the pine trees. These plants had roots, of course, when we dug them up — just ahead of the road-trimming crews — but they wilted fast and that bed of sand and peat moss back in the shade is a sort of convalescent ward.

I started it a few years ago at the suggestion of Andy Sparks as a place to root chrysanthemums and I have found that it has restorative effects on almost any plant suffering the shock of transplant. It's a crude nursery — an old door frame I hauled from the lumber pile, put down under a pine tree in a little thicket of sumac where the direct rays of the sun can't reach it and filled with peat moss and sand. If it were a bed for starting seeds I might buy builder's sand and sterilize it with boiling water and cover it with glass window panes (also salvaged from the dump) or a sheet of plastic. But I haven't gone to that much trouble for plants being moved. Sand hauled from the ditch where rainwater washes it and mixed with peat seems to suit them well enough. You will lose a few, particularly of the hard-to-move plants, but most of them will perk up and start setting new roots immediately.

They are easy to lift from this bed to a new home well prepared with woods' earth and a blanket of pine needles and oak or beech leaves — this for acid lovers and most wild flowers are.

To know how to prepare a bed for wild flowers should be easy. Just examine the spot where they are already growing and try to duplicate it, you'd think, but it doesn't always work out that way. For years I tried to transplant bird's-foot violets *(Viola pedata)*, that handsome pansy-faced charmer that grows so well in the southern mountains. I have never been able to find a sunny bank dry and arid enough to suit it. But I notice in the last few springs that colonies of these violets are coming closer, cropping up along the roadside, where they weren't before, and I hope they'll eventually show up in my yard.

Pipsissewa *(Chimaphila umellata)* is an enchanting little plant that I yearned to have in my garden somewhere. Despite the fear that it is getting to be a rare, don't-pick plant I have dug up and hauled home a few of these, trying doggedly to get them to like a shady spot by the terrace where their shiny evergreen leaves and waxy fragrant flowers could be properly seen and admired. They promptly died.

But when I started my sand and peat convalescent ward back in the woods I discovered I could hardly walk for pipsissewas growing, multiplying and blooming all over the ground under the pines. It shows you something about the independent spirit of nature's own children.

The more I see of it the more I'm inclined to stick to seeds, particularly in view of the growing scarcity of so many wild flowers and the risk involved in moving them. Few conservationists, even those who supervise the national parks, will object to your having a few seed pods in the fall. They do object, strenuously, to your moving plants.

One of the photographers who did some of the lovely pictures in _Wildflowers in Color_, a beguiling book about flowers in the Shenandoah, Blue Ridge and Great Smoky Mountain parks, told me the sad story of some rare bloomer that he had assiduously sought in mountain hollow and cove for months. Finally he found one with its buds slowly unfolding, just hours away from the exact moment of perfection. He marked it well on his mental map and decided to linger in the area and wait it out. When he returned four hours later a fat lady tourist with a shovel had just finished digging his subject up and was hauling it to her car and certain death.

He didn't beat the lady over the head with her own shovel but he wanted to and his indignation over loss of the plant to the book and to all flower lovers who visit the national parks made a profound impression on me.

We should all mind them well on the Blue Ridge Parkway when they repeat the admonition of an old ranger who begged visitors to "take nothing but pictures and leave nothing but your footsteps."

From a purely practical standpoint, it's easier to buy wild plants than to steal them. You get them at the season of the year when they should be moved and they come well rooted and conditioned for planting. If you don't know what you are looking for, that's where the national parks and forests and such public gardens as Callaway's at Pine Mountain, Georgia, can serve you. There you can see the pretties ensconced and maybe blooming, either labeled or identified by guidebooks, and decide then if you like them.

There are about a dozen wild-flower dealers around the country and your local nurseryman can probably recommend one near you. People in my area love to ride up through the Great Smokies and visit E. C. Robbins' Gardens of the Blue Ridge in Ashford, North Carolina.

The plants I got from them did very well but not nearly so well as the common chicory *(Cichorium inbus)* I got from a weed-grown lot by a filling station in Asheville, North Carolina. It is a morning bloomer, closing up its deep-blue, raylike petals about noon. I caught it early in the morning and since I grew up on the gulf coast where many people put chicory in their coffee, I was attracted by the idea of having the plant whose long tap root, when dried and ground, flavors that dark and pungent brew.

"Aw, you don't want that old pest," said the filling-station man.

I laughed indulgently. One man's weed is another man's pampered exotic, I said. That lovely blue flowering chicory didn't grow in my neck of the woods.

But it does now. Oh, it does now— —all over the place! As usual, when a wild flower does well in my garden I have but to look it up in a book to find it called: "A handsome plant and a noxious weed. Once started, hard to control."

I just hope the people of Sweet Apple settlement can be persuaded to start putting chicory in their coffee.

Chapter 10

"Among the miscellaneous miracles and shortcuts with which gardeners are confronted on every hand, a few are genuine and worth your while. For one, container-grown plants... Container plants, while not fool-proof, are more likely to be gardener-proof."

—Ralph Bailey

ONE DAY WHEN I STOPPED to buy Bibb lettuce and eggplant from my neighbors down the road, the Mansell family, I overheard the head of the household, Charlie Mansell, talking to another customer, a man.

"Yes," he sighed, "I dread it. Every morning when I get up I know I've got to face it and I dread it something terrible."

"You mean farming?" I asked, putting in my oar. He turned and faced me in blank amazement.

"Oh, no, ma'am!" he cried. "Not farming. I love to farm. I was speaking of shaving."

No doubt about it, Charles Mansell is one of our area's top farmers—a man who is making a notable success of raising truck crops when most of the old-time farmers in the county have either sold out to shopping centers and housing developers or to big operators who turn corn and cotton fields to pasture and raise horses and cattle. The Mansells grew such beautiful vegetables for supermarkets, all suburbia turned up at their back door begging to buy the surplus. As a result, they put up a circus tent over on the highway to better serve their customers and that grew into a big warehouse-sized concrete block building, where they now dispense their home-grown vegetables in season and those hauled in from the state market when production in their fields and slat houses is dormant.

It's really a business that seems to engross the entire family from sunup to sundown and I'm always amazed that they have time to personally plant, cultivate and harvest vast quantities of produce themselves.

Charles Mansell's love of farming, of course, explains it. There isn't anything on earth — or probably in heaven either — that he would rather do than work the earth.

For some of us, who also love it, there is neither time nor space nor talent nor knowledge to garden that extensively. We do it in fragments of time snatched from other enterprises on bits and pieces of earth.

The continuing wonder is how much success and pleasure gardening like this can bring.

Andrew and Olive Ann Sparks live in the city and much of their yard is given over to trees and shrubs and a flagstone terrace. Yet they raise quantities of fresh vegetables in cans set at the edge of the terrace where the sun reaches them. Tomatoes — and squash and peppers and cucumbers and even beans flourish in five-gallon cans,

which Andy collected from an oil company, cleaned and painted in bright colors. He once sold a piece to a magazine on the rewards of raising "canned vegetables."

This form of agriculture was slow to attract my attention, probably because my acquaintance with what the British call "pot gardening" was confined to window boxes and porch boxes full of coleus in my childhood and the kind of old stew kettle or chamber pot that used to turn up on front porches in the country holding beefsteak begonias, Wandering Jew or Boston ferns. The container, in that case, was often so striking that you didn't notice the plant. Caring for potted plants always seemed a *puttery* old-lady occupation to me, something to be done when you lacked the strength for real gardening. I couldn't remember to water those I had in the house and they grew limp and dusty and even when they survived they weren't anything to cheer about.

Then I noticed Roy Wyatt's tubs.

Roy Wyatt is an interesting young man who teaches German at Georgia Tech, grows all manner of flowering plants at his home in the little town of Alpharetta about six miles from me, operates a small nursery near our closest shopping center and writes a garden column for our Sunday newspaper. All this and he's always ready for a relaxed and leisurely chat about plants and planting.

His most eye-catching specialty, I think, is the way he gets maximum beauty in minimum space. He has, scattered around his nursery, a dozen or so half barrels acquired from a local barrelmaker a few years ago and they are a summer-long show of color. But I think he could plant anything in anything and it would come out looking distinguished and beautiful.

It is, of course, his artist's unerring eye for line and color and his plantsman's knowledge of the material that guide him in the selection of plants—low-growing and medium-growing marigolds, usually for a center, ringed around with purple petunias, for instance, or dwarf ageratum. (Marigold Moonshot looks good in this arrangement and so does a new one called First Lady.) He may have one tub devoted entirely to those compact, heavyheaded zinnias called Peter Pan in shades of pink and plum. (When that variety of zinnia showed up in the market early in the year I passed it up as too expensive and probably not a bit superior to the regular giants and lilliputs I always get. But I won't make that mistake again. Ah, how that little beauty blooms!)

He will have one tub devoted to begonias encircled by a marigold called Irish Lace, which has fine-cut foliage and minute creamy-white flowers. I don't particularly like

lantana, having grown up where it was a pest, but it looks beautiful in one of Roy Wyatt's barrels, surrounded by a little foliage plant called Pink Polka Dot.

He can plant prince's feather in shades of yellow or red in the center of a tub with little hot peppers set around it and the effect is stunning.

In the semishade between his office and his greenhouse he has a slatted crate that tulip bulbs came in last fall. When the bulbs were gone he lined the crate with plastic, filled it with rich dirt and planted it with coleus, a big one from a six inch pot in the center and half a dozen little ones from two-inch pots around it. The colors blend together like the jewel tones in a priceless old oriental rug and the container itself, weathered a soft gray, is interesting and effective.

After I looked at that I came home and viewed my coleus box with a different eye. The plants given me for my birthday in May by my neighbors Doc and Verda were handsome in themselves and they had certainly grown — planted as they were in practically all cow manure. But they marched along in a rather monotonous row, all the same size, with no variation except in color. If I had put them in a different-shaped planter instead of the long and skinny box, where the moonflowers are planted at the end of the porch, there would have been room for a more symmetrical arrangement. Next year I'll know — I hope.

Container planting appeals to me increasingly, not just because, as Roy Wyatt says, it is more concentrated gardening, where you have little weeding to do and your watering is all in a small area, but because it can be such an inventive way to garden. It is also fairly portable. You can have a spot of color almost anywhere you want it, limited, of course, by the sun or shade needs of your plant and your ability to enlist a strong back to help you when the housewifely urge to rearrange the tubs and crocks hits you.

So far I have limited my pot gardening to the usual geraniums and petunias in the window boxes, the hanging baskets under the eaves, a tub of rosemary by the back door, a couple of strawberry jars by the back steps and a barrel and a keg or two which brighten the shade of the terrace with bouquets of white sultana.

For a number of years I had house leek by the front stoop in two wooden tubs, which were my legacy from an old log-cabindwelling friend, Mr. Jim Whitley. One of the tubs was his washtub and the other was his bathtub and I thought that by filling them with dirt and planting them with house leek, which already grew in the cabin yard, I would preserve them for all time. Unfortunately, after five or six years the iron hoops rusted out, the staves sprang out and now the leek is back on the ground. I think I'll try again — maybe not with such log-cabin-suitable containers as wooden washtubs because I don't know where I'd find them any more, but with wooden boxes built out of cypress or cedar, if possible, and planted with something bright and cheerful and practically indestructible. That lovely Queen of Heart's dianthus, for instance, which blooms all summer, and pair it with white ageratum. Or possibly flaming spikes of dwarf salvia enclosed by cool gray artemisia.

One of Roy Wyatt's tubs contained coleus surrounded by Blue Magic and Candy Apple petunias but, as he pointed out, petunias often let you down in mid-

summer, getting seedy and bedraggled-looking and need- ing to be "renovated" and pruned back. When they're pretty they're very pretty but container gardens are no place for yes-and-no bloomers. You want something with staying qualities.

V. Sackville-West once recommended planting apple pips in a flower pot in commemoration of a birth or a christening and watching "the growth of the infant tree keep pace with the growth of the human infant." It's a happy idea, but if you're in a hurry and more interested in fruit than ceremony you might do better to buy a dwarf tree. After all, the baby has passed the seed stage and the tree might as well be up, too.

Figs take well to pots, I understand, and so do grape vines, which you can train over bamboo poles. I once read about somebody who planted a Heavenly Blue morning glory in a pot and trained it over the living-room wall, having garlands of leaves and flowers all winter. Morning glory is a dirty word in my part of the country, where it springs up in every garden and chokes out vegetables and other flowers, so I won't try that. But there are certainly other vines that would do well indoors in the wintertime and it would be fun to experiment. The perennial Con- federate jasmine with its star-shaped white flowers is a possibility.

Tubs of boxwood and ivy are standbys of city gar- dens but I don't see why they wouldn't be useful to have for country doorways in the winter when flowering plants are gone. I have often thought of starting slips of box- wood in the sand back in the woods and having some potted up to stick into the kitchen window boxes when the frost has taken the annuals.

The trouble with winter plants for the window boxes is that it would do the birds and me out of our favorite feeder. After the first killing frost is predicted — and this always sends me out by dark of night to salvage what I can in the way of plants — we cover the boxes with wide pieces of puncheon flooring and set out seeds and suet. The birds come in droves looking as colorful as rare exotic flowers and making scullery jobs on the other side of the glass not only bearable but diverting.

Finding containers suitable to your house and your plants can be a project for many interesting expeditions. I like strawberry jars, which are readily available at almost any roadside pottery or Jugtown. Old crocks and churns are pretty and set off almost anything planted in them if you can get a hole or two bored in them for drainage. (A friend with an electric drill is a godsend here.) I've had a brown and white crock in service for years — once planted with devil's backbone and now holding a pretty variety of crowfoot ivy.

Hanging baskets seem to me to be as much a part of summertime on a porch as lemonade and rockers. My mother always had them and I have them. Recently they have been upstaged by hanging thingumajigs made of plastic, which is, I'm sure, as practical as all get-out but about as pretty as a detergent bottle. Somebody came up with the idea of lining the old-fashioned wire baskets with sheets of plastic and it is a great water saver, I'm sure. You don't have to water as often or as much as what you pour in doesn't run right out. I take my baskets down and set them in a dishpan to soak periodically and for the rest of the time I think the sound of them dripping on the brick terrace sounds cool and summery. But next year

I may try the plastic sheet idea, hiding it with moss as usual. Collecting moss from the banks of a ditch down in the woods is one of my favorite April rites.

Variations of the wire-hanging basket idea can be interesting. I found the top half of a bird cage by an abandoned barn down the road and have set it aside to do something fetching—I don't know what yet. It's rather big and lightweight to fill wih dirt but I might rig up a sort of plastic pillar of peat moss and sand and manure to go through the middle and plant it thickly with many varieties of smallleafed ivy which could trail out through the bars of the cage, hiding the plastic (I hope) and making the bottom of the cage (really the top but it will hang upside down) look lush and green.

Roy Wyatt thinks it's possible to make a plastic clothes hamper or garbage can into a handsome planter. He's probably right, although I abhor plastic and notice that he himself uses natural wooden containers. At least it's worth giving it a try if you have nothing better and are eager to garden. I'm often amazed at how many things adapt themselves to planting. I once saw a rough old hog trough looking

extremely handsome loaded with pots of ferns and chrysanthemums. My mother gave me her old wall coffee mill and I thought fleetingly of putting a philodendron in it but she scotched that right away.

"You can have that coffee mill if you will use it to grind coffee," she said firmly. "If you use it for a planter or wire it for a lamp, I take it back."

It's not in daily use, as it once was, but if I have coffee to grind it's there — no dirt, no wires.

Some decorator friends of mine once grew quite a presentable tomato crop in the cheap and fragile bushel basket in which a country friend had given them rich dirt for their house plants. It didn't look substantial but it lasted the season and was quite pretty on their city terrace. (I think produce dealers still give these baskets away, if anybody is interested.)

In all of these confined gardens drainage is of the utmost importance. Gravel or shards of old clay pots are fine for the bottom layer and after that you can suit your soil to your plants. Nearly everything seems to like what Mr. Wyatt dishes up — a mixture of loam and cow manure. He adds one of the "complete" commercial fertilizers as the season progresses. My method, not sanctioned by any known authority, is to leave off the commercial fertilizer and water my tubs and jugs and baskets with a little cow manure tea in the cool of the evening.

The results are not spectacular but I've decided that it's because I have lacked Roy Wyatt's imaginative choice of plant material. Next year... ah, next year. In the meantime, maybe I should travel. They tell me that in Spain, Italy and France pot gardening is an art form and the lowliest street is made colorful by urns overflowing with beauty.

Chapter 11

"Yet not without some soul does one eat the honey of his own hives. One cannot assist his bees in all their sweet work without learning many a lovely thing among the meadows, without hearing many a sweet wild note within the woods."

— Dallas Lore Sharp

LARRY CHADWICK, scion of the old storekeeping family up on Arnold Mill Road, is a young man of many interests and enthusiasms, all of which appear to be infectious. At least, when he told me that what I needed at Sweet Apple was a hive of bees—a hive of *his* bees—I capitulated at once.

"Where are they? Can I have them now?" I asked right away.

Busy as he was waiting on customers, Larry paused to give me a quick lesson in beekeeping. You don't just grab up a hive of bees in the middle of the day and stick them in the back seat of your car and haul them home with you, he said. For one thing, workers of the hive are likely to be away at their farflung places of employment. And there was the additional matter of getting stung. Had I ever been bee stung, he asked.

Well, I've been stung by a great many members of the flying fraternity but I don't remember any bees. The reason, I told him smugly, is that I'm a very calm and tranquil person. I don't exude fear or nervousness, both of which excite bees. In fact, I suggested modestly, I am probably a natural-born beekeeper.

All the beekeepers I ever knew were quiet people. I might say, admirable people. They have been peaceable, contemplative types—farmers, philosophers, poets—eternally caught up in the mystery and beauty of life.

"Really?" said Larry distractedly, ringing up the price of a sack of fertilizer and a tractor part for another customer. "Well, my wife, Sandra, is caught up in honey. That's why I've got to get rid of some of my bees. It's all over the place in tubs and dish pans and on the kitchen

floor and in the baby's hair. Sandra says it's those bees ... or her."

It wasn't exactly the approach of Pliny or Vergil, a couple of other well-known beekeepers, but it was all right. Larry was going to give me some bees and I couldn't wait to get them.

It took several months for the bees to be delivered. That was summer and not a good time for disturbing them, Larry said. Early autumn came and the evenings should have been cool enough to drive them in to bed early so we could take the pickup truck and move them about first dark. But it was a pretty hot fall. And every time I'd call up and ask Larry if the propitious hour for bee moving had come he would say no. Like smalltown people before air conditioning, all the bees seem to gather on the front porch of the hive and fan themselves on a hot evening.

Sometime in the winter I finally got my bees. My neighbor Quinton Johnson, who used to carpenter for me occasionally, said he would take his truck and go get them first chance. And one morning before good daylight I heard Quinton's truck in the driveway and then the sound of the wheelbarrow and then the sound of Quinton running!

Despite Larry's efforts to tape up the entrance to the hive for the trip, something had joggled loose and the bees were pretty mad at finding themselves in a mobile home. They took their wrath out on Quinton.

He's not allergic to bee sting, and after he had brushed off a few stingers and applied a little tobacco juice to the wounds he came back and we edged the hive into position in the woods beyond the garden.

There began the love affair that no gardener should be denied—the cultivation of bees.

Bees are more company than beans or tomatoes and their product is without compare. At least, to the doting beekeeper. I used to be choosy about getting light honey, giving myself connoisseur airs about that which is made from the blossoms of the sourwood tree. But now whatever comes out of that hive back behind the garden is Our Own Honey and richer and prettier, more fragrant and more delicious than that which the sacred bees on Mount Dicte fed to the infant god Zeus. (You know, of course, that's why bees have so much shining gold on their bodies and in their wings? Zeus, when he finally made it to Mount Olympus, rewarded the bees for feeding him honey by clothing them with gold. The goat Amalthaea, who supplied him with his milk, was placed in the sky as the star Capella, which shows you what the rewards for social service were in those days.)

Ever since I read of a man who grew cucumbers in glasshouses in New England and had to pollinate the blossoms by hand until he hired some bees for the job, I have been certain that my garden needed bees. Then I read of California fruitgrowers who rent bees to make sure their orchards are well pollinated and I knew at once that my two apple trees and halfdozen peach trees were crying for bees.

The bumblebees and butterflies and sundry pollen gatherers and spreaders were all right in their places, but how could you be sure they were really working? With bees, there's no question. Every day the sun shines those bees beat me out of bed and if there is a flower blooming anywhere they are there, dipping into it for nectar, coming out dusted with pollen. The least impressive flowers in the yard get their loving and diligent attention. When the wild persimmon blooms I scarcely notice its flowers but the bees cover it. They fill the wild cherries with their humming and make a lyre of the pear tree.

Clearly every garden needs bees. More than the garden maybe, the gardener needs bees. Their life style is so interesting, their place in literature so entrancing, the lore and superstition surrounding them so hair-raising. All this and honey, too.

Since I read Maurice Maeterlinck's classic, *The Life of the Bee*, many years ago I have been a potential beekeeper. He made their golden cities of wax, their flower-filled world seem far too fascinating to miss.

"To him who has known them and loved them," Maeterlinck wrote, "a summer where there are no bees becomes as sad and as empty as one without flowers or birds."

Of course, I can't really see what goes on in that hive. I hope someday to invest in one of those glass-sided hives that dealers in beekeeping equipment sometimes have so I can observe their highly organized home life in operation. Meanwhile, I go out daily to check their goings and comings and to be sure they are still there.

When the weather gets very hot they are prone to congregate outside the hive and the first time I saw that happen I was sure they were swarming. I rushed to the telephone and called Larry Chadwick, who interrupted some transaction in seeds or fertilizer or farm machinery, to soothe and reassure me. That's just par for hot weather, he said.

The next time we yelled for Larry it was a bona-fide swarm. I walked out to the car on my way to work one morning and the air was full of bees, gold-winged little bodies dipping and swirling in some kind of gala holiday dance.

By midafternoon my neighbor Olivia had found them clotted in a sort of heart-shaped wedge on a pine branch at the edge of the woods. I had a spare hive, bought for two dollars at an old farmhouse auction, and Larry suggested that we put it as close as possible to the hanging cluster of bees. To make sure that it was really close, Jack and Jimmy constructed a platform out of two-by-fours right under the pine branch and set the empty hive on it.

We held hourly consultations with Larry. No matter how busy he was, this was urgent. Suppose the bees went away? Something I had read gave me the feeling it was terrible luck to be deserted by one's bees.

As long as we could see we sat on the back steps and

watched that clot of living bodies on the pine tree. When it got too dark to see we gave up and went indoors and worried.

The next morning the cluster on the tree limb was gone. There was no activity around the spare hive. I went fearfully to the old hive, expecting to mourn an empty house, and there were the workers coming and going as if nothing had happened. They had apparently enjoyed one day off from their labors and then slipped back into the old routine. Now we are waiting out the time when a new queen is crowned and the drones take to the air with her.

But you can't say bees are capricious, notional creatures. Whatever they do is part of some super plan. If they kick up their heels on a cool and shining day in June you can bet your boots they'll work overtime to make up for it.

The trouble may have been, Larry suggested, that they had filled their house with honey and were looking for new worlds to conquer. Anyway, a few days later he and another neighbor, Jim Holland, were robbing their bees and they offered to come and rob mine. I had to be in town at the time and I thought they might decide to skip my hive in their rounds of their own, but the next morning when I walked out on the screened porch there were four little television tables set up with dozens of those plastic plates they put meat in at the grocery store holding wedge after wedge of creamy comb oozing dark amber.

"The heavens declare the glory of God, and so does a drop of honey," wrote Dallas Lore Sharp in *The Spirit of the Hive*. "One can steer as straight a course by a drop of honey as by that steadfast star in the mariner's sky."

I can't, I regret to say. But I may learn. Where there's one single crop of blossoms dominating—clover or alfalfa or orange blossoms—it would be easy. We had a mountain friend, Johnny Armstrong, who used to move his bees about, treating them to sourwood in the Chattahoochee National Forest in June and July and moving on to places where the wild asters were plentiful in August and September. His sourwood honey, delicate in flavor and a pale gold in color, always took all the blue ribbons at the Georgia Mountain Fair.

My bees apparently supped from darker blossoms. I apologized when I offered some of their honey to Laura Dorsey.

"It's a little dark and sharp tasting," I said.

"Oh, that comes from the tulip poplar tree," she said. "Very choice, very nutritious."

So I spent a happy Sunday stuffing comb into fruit jars and trickling that choice and nutritious sweetness

over it. The comb, which is said to contain priceless enzymes available to all who chew it with their breakfast toast, is a constant marvel to me.

As Mr. Sharp wrote, "Defter builders than the bees I know not, or wiser; and there is a serious beauty, intellectual rather than esthetic, showing in all their work. Nowhere in nature is there an absence of this adaptation, the poetry we call fitness, which measures every line from means to end, though seldom is it so purely an intellectual expression as among bees."

Smarties that they are, bees have probably generated more superstition than any of God's other creatures. That feeling I had that it was bad luck to have them leave is an example. Ancients who also admired the comb for its intricate workmanship, its chewability and its use for candles, tried to halt a swarm by reminding the supposedly religious bees of their obligation.

"Bee, go up and bring us honey and wax!" they chanted. "Some wax for the saints and some honey for our children!"

There was a Belgian anti-swarm charm which went:

King of the bees,
Stay here in the grass,
In order to honor
The altar of the Lord
With sweet honey and wax.

The old superstition that bees have to be in on all family news is touched on in Whittier's poem "Telling the Bees." It seems that bees are very sensitive and if

they are not apprised of important events in the family—births, weddings and deaths, particularly—they will take off. In some places in Europe, I understand, the practice of "telling the bees" continues and in time of joy hives are decorated with red ribbons, in time of grief, crepe.

There was a feeling that if the bees were not informed of the death of their master they would fly up into the sky in search of him in heaven. Incidentally, the bees, alone among creatures, are widely believed to have a place in heaven next to man's.

Before a beekeeper dies it is considered proper for him to settle the fate of his bees, as he would with his children, by deciding which of his heirs will be responsible for them. The fortunate inheritor then knocks on the earth by the hives three times and says, "Little bees, Father is dead. I am your master now."

Some of my neighbors, still half-adhering to the lore their forebears brought from Britain to the Appalachian Mountains of North America, assure me that if bees are to flourish it is necessary to talk to them.

This is where I bog down. I try but after you have said, "Good morning, friends. Nice day, isn't it?" conversation languishes. I think it is because I have not learned to interpret their response. If they wagged their tails or something the way dogs do it might be easier. But bee talk is apparently on a much loftier plane and I haven't got the hang of it yet—except as they express themselves in honey.

Chapter 12

"But the ladies were not satisfied with mere talking."

—*Athens Banner* (Georgia), 1892

A FRIEND OF MINE who is ever on the alert for evidences of snobbery once told me to be very careful before joining a garden club.

"There is a *right* garden club, you know. Just as there's a *right* Brownie troop and a *right* obstetrician. Get with the wrong one and your goose is cooked socially!"

Not being inclined to worry much about my goose's social status, I laughed at her and forgot about it. Through the years, having too little time to garden and none for clubbing, I've accepted without question the popular conception of garden-club ladies as women who were more serious about meeting and eating than about tilling the soil. You can hear all kinds of horrendous tales about people's mothers winning blue ribbons at the flower show with stuff they bought from a florist and practically any married man you meet has some amusing little anecdote about "the girls" making arrangements out of poison ivy.

Practically any man except Dr. Hubert Owens, that is.

"If you are going to make garden-club members look silly," says he, "count me out."

He believes very strongly — and for good reason — that if this country continues to be a fit place for human habitation it will be due in large measure to the garden clubs.

Dr. Owens, dean of the University of Georgia's School of Environmental Design, happened to be president of the American Society of Landscape Architects and a member of President Johnson's advisory committee on beautification in 1966 when he got word that the highway beautification bill was in trouble.

A worker in the Washington vineyard called him and asked him to get the landscape architects to communicate with their congressmen.

"And do you know anybody else who can help?" asked the caller.

"Thousands!" responded Dr. Owens promptly. "The garden clubs."

Right away Dr. Owens got on the phone to St. Louis, where the board of the National Council of State Garden Clubs was in session. He held the line while a page summoned the president from the platform where she was presiding. When she came to the phone and he told her that Congress was about to reject the bill which would withhold federal monies for superhighway construction in states refusing to ban billboards, all hell, as one husband later put it, broke loose.

She went back to the platform, reported what Dr. Owens had told her and adjourned the meeting so the 150 board members could run, not walk, to the nearest telegraph office and dash off telegrams to their congressmen and to members back home who would do the same.

"I've heard since then," mused Dr. Owens, "that Western Union in St. Louis never had it better."

There were compromises, of course, but the bill passed and the nation's attention was not only focused on the need for highway beautification but two words that hadn't had much use before suddenly were on everybody's tongue — pollution and ecology. And in the forefront of the battle are women. Not the pretty little innocents who don't know poison ivy from aspidistra and go to garden-club meetings for the food and sociability, but a knowledgeable army of amateurs who are, as Dr. Owens puts it, serving as "watchdogs for America's outdoors."

Dr. Owens has every reason to be prejudiced in favor of "the girls." He lives and works in the cradle of the garden club. America's first garden club was organized in Athens in 1891 by twelve of the town's socially prominent matrons. They called themselves the Ladies' Garden Club and they met in the drawing room of one of the town's beautiful white-columned antebellum mansions, bringing slips and cuttings of plants to exchange.

Although they were well-to-do women with sizable estates and staffs to go with them, each one was apparently a serious gardener and newspaper stories of the day reveal that they began by experimenting with vegetable and flower seeds, soil treatment and insect control. Their first flower and vegetable show was held in the second

year of their organization and even if they had no classifications and no premium lists the fete apparently generated interest and enthusiasm and they were soon seeking out a horticulturist to give them some expert advice.

Garden clubbers still hunger and thirst after knowledge.

Dr. Owens, who is sort of den father to the garden clubs of the country and one of the few male members and an honorary director of several, helped the girls organize a series of landscape-design study courses. These are tough sessions, running two and a half days each in four classroom stints over a period of two years, with an additional load of outside reading.

The first ones were held at the University of Georgia and they have since fanned out to the other sections of the country—on college campuses and off—with a total of 24,000 women having enrolled in the courses at last count.

The curriculum, taught by professionals, is not easy, particularly since each course carries with it a tough exam. Beginning with a history of landscape architecture, going back to Egypt, Greece, Persia and Rome, courses include principles of design for home grounds; ecology and environment; theory and basic principles of landscape design; roadside, park and playground development; art and nature appreciation; planning and zoning; subdivision and land development conservation and many other subjects.

The idea is not to make pros of these students but to qualify them as able landscape critics who can serve intelligently as members of park boards, highway commissions, zoning commissions and school grounds committees. It is a source of some gratification to Dr. Owens to pick up a paper and read that one of these grads is serving on the mayor's committee on City Park Planning and Beautification in Utica, New York, another is on the Parks and Recreation Board of Fort Worth, Texas, and several, like Mrs. Charles Yarn of Georgia, are on their governor's advisory committee on environmental design.

Closer to home there is a constant reminder of the garden clubs' sense of public responsibility in the lovely Founders' Memorial Garden on the University of Georgia campus just outside Dr. Owens' office door. On the fiftieth anniversary of the founding of the Ladies' Garden Club in Athens the state organization decided to finance the planting of a memorial garden at what was then the School of Landscape Architecture, situated in a beautiful old rose-colored brick ante-bellum house on the edge of the campus. The school, now called School of Environmental Design, grew and eventually moved out, and the house was restored and lovingly furnished with museum-quality antiques of the period by the garden clubs as a state headquarters and memorial to the founding mothers.

The garden, really a series of gardens, is so lovely that it has been "done" at least once by most of the national gardening magazines and is visited by hundreds of garden-club members and aspiring gardeners from all parts of the nation each year. Immediately back of the house, enclosed by a white picket fence, is the formal boxwood garden centered by a sundial. I love the inscription, which reads: "Seize, mortal, seize the passing hour. Improve each moment as it flies. Life is a short summer, man a flower. He dies, alas, how soon he dies."

To put the stamp of the state's agricultural personality on the garden, the landscapers worked out in four boxwood beds the design of Georgia's most famous crops—a watermelon, a cotton boll, a peach and a Cherokee rose. In addition to this small and delightful garden there are a couple of terraces overlooking a big perennial garden enclosed by a serpentine brick wall, beyond which eight magnificent magnolia trees make a wall of glossy green leaves, muting campus and street noises.

On the other side of the house the garden, shaded by century-old oaks, runs to a natural woodland of shrubs and trees enclosed by an iron fence.

As if its beauty weren't reason enough for being, the Founders' Memorial Garden serves as an aboretum for the university's School of Environmental Design. It is important to the school as a laboratory of ornamental horticulture, essential both to teaching and accreditation.

But the garden clubs did not stop with their Founders' Garden. They are contributing handsomely to the establishment of a two-hundred-acre botanical garden for the university's use on the Oconee River — a massive effort helped along by Georgia nurserymen, landscape architects and other groups interested in the education of the young who will be charged with the future preservation of the out-of-doors.

Any time I hear the uninitiated joke about the garden clubbers as lily-handed ladies, unsullied by the soil, I think of those in Rome, Georgia. Once I carried in my newspaper column a letter from an old lady patient at the state hospital for tuberculosis sufferers. She liked the hospital and thought its lawns and trees and shrubbery fine enough. But sometimes when homesickness hit her she yearned for a place to dig in the dirt and grow a few of the common flowers of her youth.

Her letter appeared in the morning paper and before noon the women of a Rome garden club had called on the hospital administrator and asked permission to start a patients' garden of annuals and perennials. As soon as permission was granted and space found, the garden club members arrived with plants, seeds, fertilizer, tools, direction and manual labor, which they have continued to offer in bountiful supply to all patients able to work even a few minutes a day in the sunshine. In addition, for those not ambulatory or not strong enough to get outdoors, they established an indoor garden of flowering house plants, which patients can tend.

There are also garden-club-sponsored gardens at the state mental hospital and the school for the blind—not just ornamentation of the institutions' grounds but active, working gardens where patients and students themselves may dig and plant. For the mental patients it is a form of therapy, long dreamed of by the late Dr. Y. A. Yarborough, the psychiatrist who headed the hospital for many years.

"There's nothing more healing than working with plants and the earth," he once told me during the lean years when feeding and housing patients was so badly financed he couldn't hire enough doctors and nurses and had no hope of greenhouses and flower gardens.

The garden clubs, bless them, are making his dream a reality. At the school for the blind horticulture was offered as vocational training with great success. But even if it shouldn't prepare a single blind boy or girl to earn a living, the project would be justified by the pleasure it brought children who "see" little seedlings and their delicate roots and flowers with sensitive fingers. Their small fragrance gardens are a delight.

Dr. Owens, who keeps an eye on garden-club activity, has applauded the work of clubs throughout the

country in such projects as that undertaken in Center-ville, Tennessee. Here the girls turned a dump into a park, hauling off sixty truck loads of old stoves and refrigerators and planting 13,000 white pines. In Sumter, South Carolina, he will tell you, thirty-eight blighted areas were turned into mini-parks by the garden clubs. It's the same from coast to coast, garden-club members learning, working, giving.

And, as Dr. Owens adds fondly, "watch-dogging."

It may be a tad florid but it's not far wrong, the "appreciation" Mrs. Thomas Hubbard McHatton wrote in 1941 to those "twelve home-loving women" who founded America's first garden club.

"Thus, there came into being," she wrote, "the first of the countless garden clubs that today spread over the land like a benediction."

Chapter 13

THE MOST NATURAL THING for the writer of a garden book is a daybook format, geared to the seasons with a reminder in July that you mustn't keep the begonias too wet and notes in December on the planting of amaryllis. When it rains in winter that's known as harness-mending weather and you're supposed to sharpen your garden tools and scrub your clay pots to have them ready for spring planting. Some writers are ready to guide you month by month, some day by day.

I wouldn't dare.

Being a gardener who runs either shamefully behind or disastrously ahead of the seasons with forgotten or unfinished projects piling up around me on all sides, I'm not qualified to set up a when-what-how schedule for anybody else.

All I know for sure is that the earth turns, the weather changes, each season as it comes offers interest, if not always joy, content, if not always high excitement.

The following then is offered not so much in an effort to instruct as in a spirit of sharing—one happy fumbling gardener's adventures in one country year.

Winter

HEAVEN MAY HOLD RICHER GIFTS for the faithful than a sunny afternoon in January but I can't think offhand what they might be. When you are a working woman who has to go to town every day there is always a formidable backlog of chores for the weekend and only a slob would waste a Saturday lounging around the fire just reading a book when the Christmas decorations are still up.

They are still up on Sunday, too, but somehow I don't feel that I really have to do chores—at least dull and uninteresting ones—on Sunday afternoon. Once I read a book by Herman Wouk about his faith and he set forth the premise that there are practical benefits, as well as spiritual ones, to a meticulous observance of the Sabbath. A highly successful playwright-novelist, he found that resisting the pressure to work on a new play on his Sabbath never hurt production. Others worked, of course, but Herman Wouk went home to join his family in a happy and solemn observance of the Jewish Sabbath.

A time for rest and meditation is necessary to the human spirit and if you find wrestling with soggy earth on Sunday afternoon restful and restorative, why not? Besides, those peony tubers that came in the mail before Christmas . . . could they wait another day?

Peonies are new to me. We didn't have them in South Alabama where I grew up. Once my mother entered some kind of contest that involved days of research at the public library, hoping to win a thousand dollars. Instead, she won second or third prize—a sackful of peony tubers. We didn't know what to do with them and whatever we did wasn't right. They never showed themselves above ground again.

But here in North Georgia peonies seem to flourish and I was thrilled to get three new ones. Unlike the ones my neighbor Ruby Chadwick gave me in the fall, these had no leaves on them to tell me which way was up. I had planted the first one before it occurred to me that those little pink buds on it were meant to climb instead of burrow. So I went into the house, trailing mud from jeans and gloves, and looked up peonies in a book which, fortunately, had pictures. Sure enough, I had planted my first peony upside down.

It was no trouble to reverse it and when I had planted the other two I progressed to one of the pleasantest little jobs of all—mixing peat moss and sand and a little woods' earth in pots to hold some Jerusalem cherry plants Betsy and Donald Hastings brought over at Christmastime and a clump of parsley out of the garden.

It's dumb to keep buying parsley at the market if you've got a whole bed of it in the clutches of winter out in the garden, I reasoned, so I dug up a few plants and potted them for the window sill.

Will the tiny curly plants, which have been yellowed by frost and flattened by ice but persist somehow, survive in the house? I went indoors to check their chances in Gertrude Foster's valuable book, _Herbs for Every Garden._ It's a window-sill grower, all right, she says, but more than that, ah, much more than that.

Parsley has a place in herbal lore that makes it twice as interesting. For instance, the seeds were once used by men to rub on their heads to prevent baldness. Like many plants, parsley is supposed to be sown on Good

Friday, perhaps, Mrs. Foster writes, "to give it time to go to the Devil nine times and back" before it germinates. And when it comes up spottily in the garden the Devil is said to take his tithe of seed.

The sun was slipping back of the pines to the west and my shoes were damp and stiff with cold when I came in but I felt rested and refreshed. Everybody needs a warm and sunny Sunday afternoon in January.

AH, IT WAS THE FINEST SNOWFALL ANYBODY EVER SAW, Alaskans included. The earth was like a rangy, freckled tomboy transformed by her gloriously glittering white wedding gown.

Citizens of Sweet Apple settlement could tell at a glance it was going to be a school and work holiday and after a little telephoning around to check on icy hills and boggy dirt roads we rejoiced that we couldn't go anywhere and set about enjoying the day.

We bundled up, loaded our cameras and took off through the woods to see our world with its new face. After two or three miles of tramping around, engaging in unskilled and indecisive snowball battles with children, setting off barking dogs and sliding and skidding a little on banks and slopes, it was good to stop in at Don and Rita Ann Holbrook's pleasant old house for coffee and fresh-made cookies by a wood fire.

Only two cars braved our road all morning. One was equipped with chains and the other with drunks. Two jolly hiccoughing drunks chugged down the road so full of booze and good will they were practically blowing kisses

to all they saw. We learned later that they took an ill-advised turn and spent five and a half hours trying to get their car out of a ditch.

The day the thaw sets in you dread the slush but is there anything fresher or finer feeling than the air when the sun comes out and the snow starts melting and dripping off rooftops and tree branches? It seems as sweet and clean as the day the earth was made with no cloud in the sky, no faint hint of smoke or smog or impure air.

The night after our big snowfall the stars were bigger and brighter than any I've seen in months and the morning of the third day could have been borrowed from early May. When I put on my coffee I stood a minute on the back steps waiting for the water to boil and trying to decide if the pearly light was dawn or a combination of moonlight and mist rising from the snow- and rain-soaked earth.

The sun showed along the rim of the earth in the east and the moon, moving westward, paled in the morning sky. The mist gave way to a brightness that caught the raindrops on the branches of the old gray apple tree and turned them into prisms.

Errands out-of-doors were irresistible—seeds to put out for the birds, the compost bucket to empty in the garden, breakfast to serve the dogs. The walks were muddy but everything else, sky, trees, air, even the weathered logs of the cabin, seemed freshwashed and immaculate. I followed dog tracks back to the kitchen, trying to think of a line by Emerson (I believe) about the ground being "all memoranda and signatures" for those who know how to read.

NOBODY BELIEVED I'D DO IT BUT I DID. I tore down the old gray board fence erected across the back yard as a backdrop for a wondrous perennial bed I visualized there and to hide the junk that a house in the country seems to collect. The glorious perennial bed didn't show — but the junk pile did. There was something about the hard acid soil that didn't agree with anything I planted against that fence.

The red roses which were to cover it died. The stately gladioli my mother brought me from Florida to mass against it in great flaming swatches of color showed briefly one summer and then vanished.

For a little while every spring I could count on a pale row of daffodils to show briefly and one memorable summer two clumps of foxglove flowered for a time.

But mostly nothing bloomed in front of that fence and everything bloomed behind it. Honeysuckle with vines as big and tough as Cassius Clay's forearms covered everything on the ground that didn't beat them back with a shovel and then took to the trees, weighting down half my fence on the way up. The trash burner spilled out paper and bottles and cans that got into the Burn instead of the Haul can by mistake. Everything we had no immediate use for but thought we might need one day was piled there — nice big cans just the right size for something (nobody knew what), the waggledy old table that wasn't good enough to use but too good to throw away, collapsed lawn furniture, old oilcans, half an old iron bed, three-year-old bean poles. My compost pile was there too and although I loved it dearly it was no object of beauty.

It wasn't easy to decide to haul all that junk to the

county dump at Morgan Falls and tearing down the fence was a wrench. I kept thinking that, given one more chance, it might support a bower of roses.

But it's gone now. We had a burnfest, inviting in the neighbors to help us keep the fire from spreading to the broomsedge and the pine thicket on one side and the house on the other. The trouble was that we elected to do our burning when the four children, John, Bird, Ted and Sibley, were present.

Losing the fence and eschewing forever a good junk hideaway upset me enough but when the young ones started bouncing around the flame I became a nervous wreck. Visitors dropped by and I gave them a distracted and sooty greeting, my eyes on a live spark making its way toward Ted's sweater. The phone rang and we all ignored it. A passerby pulled in the driveway and honked a sociable horn at us. A little wind had sprung up and we dared not turn our backs on the fire to say hello.

When it was over we collapsed on the porch with cold drinks, feeling a little singed around the edges but accomplishing.

The scorched earth looks terrible now but come the spring...

SOMETIMES I GET HOMESICK FOR MY SHABBY OLD HOUSE in town with the kind of waste space like sleeping porches and sun parlors and pantries that profligate builders used to put in houses early in this century. But then there'll come a winter morning when I'm up in time to see the sunrise and I'm once again a country convert.

A kitchen window that looks out on woods and the rising sun is worth a great deal of driving in traffic and chafing at lack of closet space.

The little pot of chives looks perky and healthy and a new narcissus planted in pebbles last fall bloomed during the night. The old colored glass that I keep on top of the lower sash makes a rainbow that seems especially lovely in the early morning light. But those are things I could have had in my city window, if I had thought about it. It's what is beyond the window that is particularly country—the sweep of brown grass, the hill rising beyond the big oak tree and the spare brown and gray beauty of the winter woods. I didn't have peach trees for the birds in the city either.

The birds' Christmas tree, inspired by Mrs. Lewis Gordon and other members of the Atlanta Bird Club, is a big success. Some people think the peach tree looks incongruous with pine cones dipped in melted suet and studded with birdseed hanging from its branches but the birds don't seem to question this strange fruit. They even find it fitting that there's half a coconut hanging there by a green wool bow—a Christmas gift from a bird-loving neighbor.

At first I thought the birds would prefer the security of a stationary feeder but they apparently love to bat the swaying cones with their beaks, grabbing seeds and suet on the wing. The little birds, titmouse, nuthatches and juncos, light on the cones and baskets made of grapefruit rinds and feast on raisins and peanut butter. One beautiful big redheaded woodpecker spent ten minutes sort of lounging on a branch and eating from a cone that the wind had wound around until it was within easy reach.

The mockingbirds and the cardinals, too heavy to light on the tree ornaments, pretend they are hummingbirds and eat poised in mid-air. They come in great numbers in the early morning, complaining like high-paying guests if the water in the shell on the terrace is frozen and I haven't replenished it. So I grab the teakettle, without even saving out coffee water, and rush out.

Maybe the most interesting thing about a country kitchen window is that it invites you outside.

A GARDENING FRIEND OF MINE, who is normally in complete accord with whatever projects his wife launches in their beautiful yard, complained the other day that one more month of winter weather and she'll bankrupt him.

"All she has to do is to sit indoors and think of things she wants to have done outside," he said. "She's even started making a list and the last time I looked it was longer than the one she made at Christmas."

Of course, it is. And he should be glad because the dreaming in winter's sit-by-the-fire months is likely to be very practical. That's when you think of broken pipes, for one thing, and resolve to take steps to protect the outside faucets better. If you've already done that, there's the water line that you'd love to have run to the garden. I got one this year and it turned out to be amazingly inexpensive. The ditch was the problem but we didn't make it too deep because we used plastic pipe and we will always cut off the water when the garden is put to bed for the winter before the last hard freeze.

My biggest wintertime dreaming runs to greenhouses. I want a greenhouse the way some women want emeralds. For a long time I wrote to every manufacturer who offered a catalogue ad in any gardening magazine, hoping that sooner or later I'd find one I could afford.

There are many that are handsome and really reasonable, as such things go, but not inexpensive enough to be out of the realm of dreams. Our neighbors Doc and Verda built themselves one a couple of years ago, attaching it to one end of their house and equipping it with louvered glass windows and a sliding, aluminum-framed glass door. It is neat and clean and conservatory beautiful with blooming house plants and a spotless flagstone floor.

But what I want is something bigger and grubbier — a place where I can start seeds early and maybe install one of those mist machines for coaxing cuttings to root. It could have a dirt floor so that dropped seeds, particularly those of shade lovers, would spring up under the benches, and maybe a pebble walkway to retain the moisture. Roy Wyatt has several homemade, inexpensive plastic houses of this kind and has promised to help me build one when I decide what I want and where.

Don Hastings offers further hope. He and a friend, young Jimmy Furniss, built quite a serviceable A-frame greenhouse of treated two-by-sixes and plastic in a single day. The cost was slightly under $100, including the deposit on a butane tank to supply the secondhand gas heater he picked up somewhere. Water is supplied by a hose from the house.

With such examples as these to inspire, with so much help offered, it would be silly not to dream with graph paper and a building-supply catalogue at hand.

Spring

Sometimes Mother Nature gives you an absolutely smashing surprise — snow in March, if you please. Maybe they are accustomed to such elegant caprices a bit farther north but in this section of the South it's the most marvelously contradictory thing the weather has done in years. Peach blossoms, pear blossoms, plum blossoms, hyacinths and daffodils and picture-book snowfall to boot.

It happened that I had to linger at home anyhow the day this wondrous phenomenon struck Sweet Apple and it couldn't have been lovelier. The kitchen is really the proper place to be when great fat flakes are covering the landscape outside.

Day in and day out I go along taking my kitchen for granted, scarcely seeing it and if I do look at it I'm prone to note that it needs cleaning up and I haven't the time for that. Then one day I see it: The silver light reflected from the snow outside picking up the brown jug of daffodils on the window sill, the little gray pitcher of rosemary and southernwood on the table, the gleam of a copper pot, the blackness of an iron skillet, the rough pine walls.

Somehow dawdling in the kitchen rocker in the middle of the morning makes a woman think food thoughts. You should be preparing something slow-cooking and savory. There seems no limit to the things you can do in this lovely space of indoor time, when you don't have to go anywhere, when nobody is likely to come to call. You hear the wind rustling in the chimney, birds fluttering to and from the bird feeder and the hum of the furnace working overtime. There isn't another sound in all that strange and beautiful white world.

It's fun to make bread on such a day. To warm the flour and shortening a bit in the oven, to get out mixing bowl and pans, to set the yeast bubbling with a bit of ginger, to sift and measure and stir and knead. My friend Margene Downs hates the mystical to-do people make over homemade bread. She makes it often and well. But there is an anonymous poem I like to think of on such a bread-making day. It goes:

> _Be careful when you touch bread._
> _Let it not lie uncared for — unwanted._
> _So often bread is taken for granted._
> _There is much beauty in bread;_
> _Beauty of sun and soil,_
> _Beauty of patient toil —_
> _Winds and rains have caressed it,_
> _Christ often blessed it._
> _Be gentle when you touch bread._

The daffodils some other woman's hand planted years ago have sprung up in all the wrong places — in the middle of the front yard where there should be lawn, at the edge of the garden and down the slope where the septic-tank-drain field will send tall lush grass up to need mowing soon. They are bright and brave, those daffodils, and whatever ideas I had about digging them up and concentrating them in one area under the oak tree or along the front bank go a-glimmering. Let them stay where they are and return every March and challenge winter's hold on the earth.

The birds have urgent errands about the yard, meetings down in the plum thicket where the honeysuckle has made a fine tangle for nesting, and songs to sing from the top of the persimmon tree.

It won't be long until the mockingbirds take over and make croaking amateurs of all the other singers. I heard a mourning dove down in the woods the other day and when I walked back to see if the bees were up and busy I heard the hammering of a woodpecker on a lightning-struck pine.

The garden under its layers of decaying branches and stems and kitchen garbage looks a little like a city dump but the young perennials don't recoil from such untidiness. The gray-green clumps of cornflowers are back in the paths again. Lacy leaves of larkspur have come up among eggshells and orange rinds and I think the poppies may be coming back. It's time to buy seed. I wonder what I did with those flats I had on the back porch last March.

IT'S BEEN MY EXPERIENCE that kite flying is not one of the simple pleasures — not the way men do it. It is a complicated engineering feat, a mystical rite, an aerodynamic puzzle best solved by Lockheed.

And yet in Sweet Apple settlement it is very big these days. Some of our neighbors have even inaugurated the custom of an annual kite-flying fete replete with hot dogs and beer. And almost any windy weekend afternoon in March, men and boys who might be more profitably occupied planting English peas and Bibb lettuce and hauling off garbage may be seen galloping madly over pastures towing kites behind them or standing on a tree-less hill holding a string and staring skyward with joy and pride.

My daughter Susan rummaged around in the rag bag looking for an old sheet to tear into strips for a kite tail and I tried to explain to her how it was going to be. The men in the family, even then kneeling on the living-room floor, would talk a lot about bridles and tails before they got anything done. When they finally got a kite in the air they wouldn't like the way it flew and would bring it down for more or less bridle and tail. It was possible the kites would land in the trees anyhow but if they didn't and flew superbly the men wouldn't let the little boys have anything to do with them.

Forewarned, Susan decided to spend the afternoon in the hammock with a book. But I couldn't resist Denver Cox's cornfield on a spring afternoon. The ground had just been turned but was not planted. The only trees were acres away and downhill. The sun was hot, the breeze strong and frisky and the view lovelier than I had dreamed. Sweat Mountain stood up sharp and blue on one side and we got a different perspective on the familiar houses that line the road on the other.

The kites cooperated and the little boys were ecstatic when they went so high it was necessary to add one ball of twine and then a second one. For a while all of us watched the dancing triangles and owned a piece of sky.

SOME GOOD GARDENERS I KNOW have about given up the

practice of starting their own seed. They point out that plants come so cheap these days — often thirty-eight cents for a flat of salvia already inches tall and showing sturdy little scarlet flags — that it hardly pays a busy person to bother with seed. They are right, I'm sure. It's time-consuming and messy filling all those little boxes and bowls and pots that I have arranged around the screened porch, back of plastic every spring, and watering and turning them and watching them.

But would I miss it? Only if I lost both of my hands in some hideous accident. For there's pure sensuous pleasure in handling seeds and soil. There's suspense and excitement in watching the little commas of green punctuate the surface of sand and peat. There's satisfaction in nursing them to the point where they can go out into the world and stand alone in bed and border.

Someday, when I get that greenhouse, I can prepare pots and flats in indoor comfort from the bins of peat and sand that I will have under the potting bench. But now I find myself on the rawest and windiest day in March kneeling by the garbage cans in the back yard sifting sand through an old screen. It's not bad work. The wind pulls at your jacket. Your jeans get damp and cold about the knees. But the sand feels good trickling through your fingers and the peat, miraculously kept dry in the shed, mixes well with it.

One part sand, one part peat, one part loam... I hum it to myself as I work, pleasantly conscious of the rattle of seeds in my jacket pocket.

Here the herbs and there the flowers. Here the peppers, there the tomatoes. Plant plenty of basil this time. I forgot to plant it last year and the garden, the larder and the flower containers were noticeably poorer. It's one of the most fragrant and most useful of the herbs and this year, I think as I sow the tiny seeds, I'm going to try drying it for winter use.

John Gerard, author of the most ancient herbal I've seen (1597) said it better: "The smell of Basill is good for the heart and for the head ... The seed cureth the infirmities of the heart, taketh away sorrowfullness which commeth of melancholy, and maketh a man merry and glad."

WHEN IT COMES TIME TO REFILL THE HANGING BASKETS in the spring I'm always glad because it's an excuse for dawdling along the creek bank. I suppose a really strongminded person could just say, "I'm off to dawdle along the creek bank" and do it—but have you ever noticed how men need fishing poles in their hands and women take along a basket and a trowel so any random observer will understand that they have a mission?

Anyhow, the hanging baskets plainly needed to be refurbished. They've been stuck in the house all winter and they looked it. Except for a weekly dousing in the kitchen sink and an occasional shifting to expose another side to the light from the window they've had little attention. The dirt was packed hard, the moss which lines them was dark and dry and the little wild ferns which did so well when they hung in the shade of the well house last summer were shriveled. Only the Wandering Jew survived and it was limp and pale.

So we took trowels and shovels and a tub and baskets and went down to the creek in search of the soft green moss which covers the banks like a lush carpet. The shovels weren't much use in getting the moss. They get involved in tree roots and you end up taking more earth than you need. We even got two spring lizards without knowing it. But if you are patient and work slowly you can loosen a corner of a swatch of moss with your hands, slip them under it and peel off almost enough to line a basket without tearing it.

This is pleasant work. It's beginning to get shady down on the creek bank—the light, pale green shade of early April. And so many flowers are coming into bloom— tiny baby bluets looking like forget-me-nots in the moss, foam flowers with their elegantly notched new leaves coming out of a rosette of winter-bronzed ones, lady slippers and hepaticas.

The ferns are coming back and sometimes I think they are the prettiest and most varied of wildings. Within a few feet I counted six different kinds, all green, all lacy with new fronds slightly streaked with silver, ready to unfold.

The little creek we visit has a spring at its head. (Once this was the site of a whiskey still and we still find rusting oilcans half hidden in the leaves.) There's a rocky waterfall with a fine granite shelf for sitting and you can cool your feet in the creek and smell spring all around you.

The sweet shrub must be at its very best now, every stem studded with fragrant little dark-red flowers. The wild azalea comes in waves—the pale pink first, the flame colored next and the white last—so there's some blooming and perfuming the air for weeks.

Up the hill in the sunlight the sweet William is a mass of pink. The tub of moss is heavy and the sun is hot on your neck and shoulders as you toil upward with your booty. But you feel as rich as if you'd been digging for gold and found some. Everybody ought to dawdle along a creek a little while in April.

GOOD FRIDAY CAME EARLY THIS YEAR and we didn't get the garden planted. I worried about it until I saw Hoyt Crowe up at Chadwick's store dipping up a measure of seed corn.

"Aren't you late with that?" I asked.

He shook his head.

"Martins are the early birds," he grinned. "Crowes don't plant until May. Got to wait for the ground to warm up."

It seems warm to the touch. We raked back the mulch and used the rototiller to turn the earth. Next year I hope we won't have to do that. Following the lead of organic gardeners and good mulchers we should have soil so loose and friable plowing won't be necessary. My soil is improving but the mulch still isn't as deep as it should be and that red clay base can be as hard as concrete.

But it looks beautiful where the blade turns it and, determined to be orderly, I got out strings and stakes and marked off straight and soldierly rows of beets, carrots, onions and beans. The trouble was the children and the dogs helped me and I won't be a bit surprised to see all the seeds coming up in one great mass like a raw and earthy goulash.

While we were about it we made hills for the Texas watermelons and cucumbers an editor friend sent us and I'm going to plant them by the moon. Charles Mansell used to plant everything by the moon but his operation became so big he now starts a lot of his garden truck in one of his big plastic covered sheds.

"Uncle of mine had the prettiest watermelons in this part of the country," he told me. "He always planted them on the first full moon in May. Even if it was raining so hard he mired up in the field he got his watermelon seeds in the ground on that day — the first full moon in May."

It was raining this year, too, and we were all heading down to Florida to spend Mother's Day with Muv but daybreak caught me in the garden in boots and raincoat planting my watermelon seeds.

THERE ARE SPRINGS AND SPRINGS. The almanac has an official one. Then there is the personal spring, the unofficial, purely private one that comes to each of us, sometimes early, sometimes late. It may be that the younger you are the earlier it comes. I have seen little boys take off their shoes and wade in ditches on an unseasonably warm day in February, absolutely convinced that spring had arrived. And I have seen old people who marveled that the first day of May could be so chill and wintry.

For me spring comes when I kneel on the ground with a trowel in my hand, feel the sun on my back and breathe in a special earthy smell that promises warmth and life.

Summer

The new window boxes were made out of redwood and I rushed out with brush and gray stain to paint them as fast as possible. Why paint redwood, my neighbors asked, why not let it age? In time it would turn to silver and blend with the gray of the logs and the batten-board kitchen wall.

"I hate redwood," I said and was immediately sorry.

Why should you hate one kind of building material, particularly a natural one like redwood? The fact that it is more indigenous to a Hollywood movie star's patio than to a log-cabin kitchen window box shouldn't make any difference. Glass and screen wire and tin for the porch roof are really as foreign to Sweet Apple as teak.

No, these little prejudices are ridiculous and I'm going to root them out of my system as ruthlessly as I wrest bindweed from the bean patch. Take purple petunias. It's idiotic the way I dislike them. Purple is becoming to violets and wisteria and lilacs but in a petunia, particularly a double petunia, it seems to me to be a horrid, floozy color.

So wouldn't you know that the flat of petunia plants I brought home for the window boxes would contain one white and six purple ones? When I finished setting out the plants I discovered the tag. That white one that was blooming got into the batch by mistake while the sneaky purple ones laid low, not showing their colors.

If it hadn't been nearly dark I might have gone out and pulled them up and given them to somebody who LIKES purple petunias. Instead, I poured myself a cup of coffee and sat on the steps where I could see the single white bloom and gave myself a lecture. All flowers are beautiful and a double purple petunia is the splendid fulfillment of some hybridizer's dream. Be glad you have purple petunias and just hope that all the cow manure you put in the boxes won't kill them.

Actually I wouldn't much care if those purple petunias expired but I have an idea that the perversity that latches on to plants at times will cause them to flourish like the green bay tree. And the funny thing about gardening is that the moment you have success with some plant it immediately becomes dear to your heart.

So it may be with purple petunias. If those little plants push their roots into that fine rich cow manure, take a running start and overflow my window boxes with dark green foliage and purple blossoms I may become a purple petunia addict. In fact, redwood window boxes with purple petunias might become my trademark. Ugh!

MY NEIGHBOR QUINTON JOHNSON was out and about early, stopping by for a minute on his way to consummate a beagle deal with another neighbor, Homer Dangar. We talked a minute on the screened porch about fishing, the way turtles are taking over certain lakes and, naturally, the weather.

"Going to be another scorcher," is the standard greeting in the country these days.

"Think it'll ever rain?" is the standard response.

After that, custom and mutual interest dictate that you take up the matter of what the weather is doing to gardens. Will the corn make? Who has ripe tomatoes yet?

Getting any beans or are they parching in the pod?

Quinton took off and I stood a moment looking at the puppies tumbling about the yard in an ecstasy of early-morning playfulness. Their pleasure in the morning is always infectious but as the sun climbs higher and the day expands they grow tired and drowsy and retire to the shade of the well house or the boxwood and collapse in a plump fuzzy pile of ears and tails and big puppy feet.

Somehow these June days affect me the same way. The mornings are lovely — cool and dew-damp and sweet with birdsong. I tiptoe out of the house with my second cup of coffee, hoping not to alert the puppies, but it is a vain hope.

They hear the squeak of the screen door and the sound of my sneakers on the rock step and they come tumbling out to greet me, barking joyfully and nipping at my ankles and wriggling delightedly between my feet so that walking is hazardous.

We have a squash plant that I have been waiting on hand and foot. It grows rampantly on the gulf coast and in Texas, stringing pecan trees with great green squashes the size of gourds like so many beads, and is delicious stuffed with shrimp and baked. A friend who runs an herb farm in Houston gave us the seed and I've been trying to get that squash to climb up on the big clothes-line out beyond the garden. Twice a day I take it a bucket of water as if I were watering a faithful horse. This has caused it to green up and reach smartly for the clothes wire. But it may not survive the attentions of the puppies. They insist on going with me to water the squash and as the water trickles down near its roots they lap thirstily at its leaves and paw the damp ground as if it harbored some ferocious beast.

No need to remind them that they have plenty of cool drinking water elsewhere or to scold them. This just causes them to turn suddenly shy and cower against the squash vine as if somebody was going to beat them. It's easier to pick them up bodily and haul them off under the apple tree, where they roll on the grass and wrestle mightily with the little green apples, which seem to be falling in greater numbers this June than ever before.

While the puppies do battle with the green apples I make my getaway, hiding indoors so they won't see me and hurl themselves against the porch screen. From the back door I can look at the day in relative tranquillity, watch the comings and goings of the brown thrashers who have a nest in the muscadine vine at the edge of the woods, admire the hummingbird's swift passes at petunias and smell the warm, slow-ripening greenness of the June earth.

Within an hour it will be too hot to venture out without a sun hat and within two hours, like the puppies, you won't want to venture beyond the deepest shade you can find, preferably air-conditioned shade.

JESS BIRDWELL, THE QUAKER NURSERYMAN IN JESSAMYN WEST'S lovely book, *The Friendly Persuasion,* spent some time listening to the rain, enjoying the notion that a blind man can tell the seasons just from the difference in the rain's sounds. Summer rain, he said, falling on trees and bushes heavy with leaves, is bound to sound different from winter rain falling on bare branches and sluicing down spare, dark trunks.

It's been so long since we've seen rain, real rain at Sweet Apple that I despaired of testing Mr. Birdwell's theory. In six weeks it has rained all around us — as close as Chadwick's store and Ebenezer Church. At Sweet Apple we've had a considerable show of thunder and lightning and enough raindrops to hit the tin roof of the porch and make a sound like a child throwing a handful of gravel up there. But that was all. No blessed cooling wetness, no invigorating draught for the parched earth, no cleansing, musical bath for the trees.

All up and down our settlement corn is shriveling in the field, grass is browning, tomatoes blistering and rotting under the brassy sun. In the morning, refreshed by a heavy dew, my zinnias and marigolds look fairly perky and the dauntless okra marches along its short rows looking like sturdy little green umbrellas. But by the middle of the day everything wilts and by nightfall fields and garden spots and flower borders are limp and bedraggled. We water a little — the hanging baskets and new young plants that are as yet unaccustomed to the rigors of summer sun — and all the time we listen to the whine of the pump in the well, wondering how long the water will hold out.

The other day it looked like it might really rain. There was a dark cloud in the east that seemed to be spreading. A wind started up in the pine trees and moved down to the persimmon and the big apple tree, skipping to the maple by the well house and the ash opposite it, tossing its pinnacles of white blooms about like blown seafoam.

The lawn mower was out and I left it out to tempt

the kind of reluctant shower that comes only when you're unprepared. I would have sacrificed a line full of drying clothes to the rain if I'd had one ready. But all I could do was take a seat on the porch and watch and wait.

The rain came...almost. For a few minutes it was there in the air—a faint fragrant mist that whispered in the tired and thirsty green leaves. Then I heard it on the roof, not drumming, not whooshing but a faint dusty rattle, tentative and almost intangible. After a few minutes its scent was all around me—the dust-stirring smell of hard drops hitting grass and walks and then the pungent smell of wet mint.

The sun-faded bricks of the terrace were not wet but patterned with stars of wetness. The rain stopped almost before it began. I picked up the watering can and went out—Jess Birdwell's theory still untested.

SOMETIMES I THINK HE'S A POET, this grizzled old farmer. Fifty years of toiling to wrest a living from rocky, hillside fields haven't taken the edge off his sense of wonder and joy in the earth and the seasons. He sows a few flower seeds in the rows with his beans and corn and lets his fence rows grow thick and ragged to offer a cover for birds. His milk cow wears a bell, not because she wanders and he has to find her, but because he and she like the pretty sound it makes.

He paints his chicken houses pink and blue because those colors "set off" white leghorns best.

The other day he was talking to me about "odd hours." He likes to feel and hear the movement of time, he said, in the ticking of the old clock on the kitchen shelf, the color of the sun and the wheeling and shifting of the stars at night.

"But best of all, I like the odd hours," he said.

"Do you mean odd-numbered?" I asked. "Like five, seven, nine and eleven?"

He laughed tolerantly.

"Well, them, too," he said. "But what I was mainly speaking about was the hours you come up on unexpectedly. Like doing something out of order and at a different time of day. Picking peas at sundown or going fishing on Monday. Try it yourself some time. People make a mistake to live their lives like one of them little bitty mules that used to pull the carts in coal mines, sticking blindly to the same track."

Later when I had one of those sleepless nights that come to everybody I thought of him. Three o'clock in the morning in the back yard is an odd time — lonely and beautiful.

The peaches are dropping off the old trees now, pretty and rosy cheeked but hard as hickory nuts. They fall with a soft "plunk" in the tall grass. A dark-winged bird stirs in the pines at the edge of the yard, a whippoorwill sounds his plaintive, questing cry back in the woods. The air is cool and sweet and whatever it was you were worrying about is diminished by the moment.

A FRIEND OF MINE USED TO PLAN to have a complete mental and physical collapse every August. She said it was an evil and an ornery month, meaning no good to anybody, especially to her, and she attributed every unpleasant thing that happened to her to "this awful old August."

Looking back I realize my friend's difficulty was that she wasn't much of a gardener. To those of us with a patch to tend August can be a very satisfying month. A month of excesses, undoubtedly, too much sun, too much heat; rain, if it comes at all, not a gentle soaking shower but a bombardment, accompanied by the flash and roar of heavenly artillery.

The subtlety of spring and early summer is not for August. Instead of the shy violets and the sweet and understated lilies of the valley we get great gaudy marigolds and zinnias, sunflowers and flaming salvia. I have never been partial to crape myrtle but in August you have to love them, the smooth silverbarked trees holding buxom bouquets of watermelon pink, magenta and old rose all along roadsides and suburban streets.

I haven't checked with my friend recently about her aversion to August but the next time I see her I must beg her to try to enjoy it. It's the last we have of summer, rich and ripe and overblown but a time to savor before September comes edging in with cool nights and chilly mornings, bringing us fall.

Fall

The days are hot in the country and sometimes the night coolness doesn't come until along toward morning. And yet in spite of the heat there's an undeniable tinge of autumn in the air.

The few leftover fireplace logs that I have stored under the shed seem to harbor some kind of insect that goes "scratch-scratch" with such an industrious sound it makes me wonder if it is sawing up winter wood for itself.

The Queen Anne's lace, which adorned dusty roadsides and weedy meadows like a dainty frill, has almost gone, giving way to the dried bird's-nest-shaped seed pods. Small purple spikes of heal-all are everywhere. Goldenrod is blooming, dogwood and sourwood show a few red leaves and somehow the purple asters that I mistakenly planted too close to the marigolds have worked their way up through the competition and haunt a few lovely shaggy blooms.

The vegetable garden is a show that has completed its run, except for the lush green rectangle of turnips, mustard and kale. Before the rains came my neighbors with big pastures were engaged in fragrant haying operations. We had our own small-scale day of haying, the children and I. We hitched the little red wagon to the back of the riding mower and hauled it about the yard, filling it with clippings of grass, which grows rank and tall down over the septic-tank-drain field.

My young helpers weren't interested long in raking the hay and loading it in the wagon but they did enjoy piling on it for a ride to the barn — the mound at the edge

of the garden, from which I will parcel it out as winter blankets for the put-to-bed plants a little later.

The spectacle of a red wagon being towed over the yard by a power mower isn't exactly a Currier & Ives rendition of autumn but the sun seemed tawnier than usual to me as it slanted across the children's path, the dried grass smelled sweet and I thought I detected the cool breath of a new season blowing up from the hollow.

COMPANY WAS COMING FOR SUNDAY-NIGHT SUPPER on the porch and I was out early scavenging for bouquets. Why is it the flowers are always having a lapse when you need them? After I had filled a basket with zinnias for the supper table, put sunflowers in the old brown pitcher for the mantel and made a bouquet of tiny pink roses (Cecile Brunners) in my great-grandpa's shaving mug for the bathroom I had run out. Or so I thought.

There is new—to me—cut-flower treasure in the double althea. The single ones fold their petals almost the minute you pick them but Muv discovered in a flowerless interim that double ones cut and keep well. The little tree I planted last year didn't need pruning exactly but I snipped half a dozen of its gardenia-like ruffled white blossoms and combined them with spikes of blue salvia in the old tea-leaf sugar bowl.

It may not have stunned my guests with its elegance but every time I passed it on the kitchen table I eyed it with pleasure.

Blue salvia is also a very satisfactory plant, more

sedate than the raucous red and so prettily shaped it combines beautifully with almost any flower you have, pink roses especially. It also dries well (I cut it, tie it in bunches and hang it on the kitchen wall until I'm ready for it), keeping its color faithfully. Best of all, it is a perennial, coming back reliably each spring to the delight of bees and butterflies.

"YOU KNOW WHAT THEY SAY ABOUT A WOMAN who goes from house to house wasting the neighbors' time," Muv said. "They say, 'She VISITS.'"

We laughed over that but it seems perfectly true nowadays that nobody can spare the time for sitting and chatting. In this day when women work outside the home and men are caught up in do-it-yourself building and gardening projects there seems to be far less time than there was before the advent of the so-called age of leisure.

In the days before labor-saving devices, Muv pointed out, all the work was done by Friday — the house shining, the yards freshly swept, the baking done, all the meeting clothes crisp and clean and waiting for Sunday, shoes polished and even, I suppose, the horses curried and the buggy cleaned.

Now washers and dryers run all day Saturday and Sunday. Housecleaning goes on all weekend and legions of men spend Sunday afternoon washing their cars and cutting the grass.

With winter coming on there should be patches of indoor fireplace time when company is very welcome. But I don't know. As long as the frost holds off, the yard is as full of assignments as a new city editor.

"Anybody who comes to see me and is physically able can expect to dig a hole or pull a few weeds," Muv remarked as we sat on her back steps. She said it apologetically and I thought I caught her alternately eyeing the hoe by the toolhouse door and my idle hands.

SOME GARDENERS, MORE RUTHLESS THAN I, have seen the handwriting on the wall for summer and have cleared their garden spot of all the limp and fading vegetation. With admirable decisiveness they have cut down and uprooted bean and pea vines and the spotted and leggy old zinnias, the going-to-seed marigolds and the tired and desiccated cosmos and petunias. In their place they have a clear, clean piece of ground newly planted to winter greens, lettuce and onions.

Much as I admire such forthright action, I can't do likewise. I'm too reluctant to let summer's lingering beauty go. One of the things about September is that you never know when summer-weary plants will take a new lease on life and bloom again before frost. Once, I remember, nasturtiums languished and played hard to get all summer—to burst into brilliant bloom in October. So I wait, snipping the dead heads from the zinnias when I think of it, listening to the insect symphony in the woods and dreaming over pictures of bulbs in the seed catalogues.

In spite of the heat the signs of fall are unmistakable. For several weeks now my neighbors have had sawhorses up and lengths of tin roofing stretched across them in the yard—drying apples for winter's pies and turnovers. The vinegary smell of pepper relish a-making is almost a palpable presence in the air. The day lilies have seed pods instead of blooms on them and michaelmas daisies, so self-effacing since last fall that I forgot them, have come to life in a blaze of blue.

Even as summer dies there are hostages to fortune to be seen everywhere. The lilac I planted by the window, thinking of Walt Whitman's "When lilacs last in the door-yard bloom'd," has never bloomed itself but I've counted six little new plants beneath it. Maybe next spring its progeny will produce.

THE *CATHOLIC DIGEST* HAD A PARAGRAPH about a four-year-old urging her busy mother to stop work and go for a walk with her.

"Stop working, Mother," she pleaded. "Let's go outside and get some use out of the world!"

Anybody not bedridden, blind or otherwise immobilized who stays indoors these days is a stone fool. The air is cool and sweet and October scented and you owe it to yourself, if not to a child you love, to "get some use out of the world."

The little boys, John and Ted, had the same idea and somehow persuaded their mother to bring them to the country. There wasn't anything in the house for a real picnic but I hastily made butter and honey sandwiches and put a few apples in a bag. We took our favorite walk to Johnson's rock on the river, down a rambling old woods road which is too rough for automobile traffic and therefore perfect for hikers.

Trees arch over the road and there's one spot where a thicket of young sassafras trees took a stand like a medieval army in blazing gold armor. The little mitten-shaped sassafras leaves turn bright red usually but here they were almost uniformly gold, except for the few that were freckled with brown. The fragrance of muscadines was still in the air, although the ones we found still clinging to the vines were overripe. Occasionally we found a hickory in full color dropping a few nuts.

A big gray rock, medallioned with gray-green lichens, is wedged into the hillside overlooking the river and that's where we sit to eat our sandwiches, listen to the wind in the tops of the trees and rest our eyes on the blue peaks of the mountains in the distance.

It was the most accomplishing weekend I've had since last October.

CLEMATIS IS NOT AN EASY PLANT for me and yet I yearn after it as one of the storybook flowers. The day I left for England on my vacation the white Duchess of Edinburgh that I planted to hide the clothesline post—the one near enough the house to be seen from the porch—had six saucer-sized white blooms. I doubted if I would see anything in all Great Britain more gorgeous. Bigger, sure. Covering acres of ancient stone walls, of course. But six blooms on your own clematis vine by your own clothesline post...well, you couldn't really beat that.

When I came back three weeks later my clematis was brown and shriveled and apparently dead.

"I watered it every day," said my daughter Mary. "I think it died of a broken heart."

I didn't tell her then that some plants don't need to be watered every day. I just mourned and watched. And I was rewarded by seeing a tiny green tendril come back. Now I think I know what the trouble was. Clematis likes to have its roots in shaded soil. I put a rock or two on it and the clothesline post is now covered with loops and swirls of green and a few late-blooming flowers.

CHRYSANTHEMUMS ARE *SUCH* NICE FLOWERS. If you tried to raise those showy football corsage blooms they might give you trouble. But if you just want something bright and fallish for late color in the beds and borders and trustworthy flowers to cut for the house, you hardly have to lift a finger with mums. I started with maybe six plants—a couple of bronze ones and a yellow one or two from the nursery, a pink a mountain friend hauled out of her basement and gave me one snowy day and a white left over from a stay in the hospital.

Andy Sparks, who used to specialize in chrysanthemums when he had a bigger yard, suggested that I snip off the terminal branches in early summer, dip the ends in a rooting compound and put them in my propagating sand bed back in the woods. To my surprise a hundred of them lived.

After I set out as many as I had space for I gave away dozens and I still have some in pots coming on for house blooming later, I hope. They have made fine sturdy, well-branched plants, requiring little attention all summer, except watering on the driest days and pinching back the buds early in the season when they hankered to bloom too soon. Now when all else is gone the mums and the blue ageratum are a tide of color across the yard.

A CRICKET SET ME TO THINKING OF EDNA ST. VINCENT MILLAY. As I knelt on the ground planting crocuses and daffodils for next spring's bloom I heard a loud singing nearby. I finally found the source and it was no bigger than a carpet tack—a little fellow swaying on a blade of grass and singing a last tune before winter.

There is a Millay sonnet about "the insistent cricket in the grass" and I went in the house to look it up. It's one from her book _Mine the Harvest,_ which was published after her death in 1950, and it is suitable to this time of year, speaking of "Tranquility at length, when autumn comes."

"Autumn stays the marching year one moment," she says, and that's a time to "compute, refute, amass, catalogue, question, contemplate and see."

In this time of violence and protest it's good to pause one autumnal moment and remember that Miss Millay, born nearly eighty years ago, was a spokesman for the liberated young people of the 1920s, a marcher and a protester on many fronts. She knew well the tumult in the minds of the young, who even then were seeing through the hypocrisies of their elders. But I think she must have had patience with mankind to have written of "Man, with his singular laughter, his droll tears/ His engines and his conscience and his art."

THIS IS A GREAT YEAR FOR WILD PERSIMMONS. What Euell Gibbons calls "the sugar plum tree" is loaded with luscious fruit, so heavy and so sweet it is falling fast and if you don't hurry the dogs will beat you to it. I didn't know that dogs were persimmon eaters until I went out walking with the Sweet Apple kennels crowd the other day along about twilight and ended up fighting them for fruit that fell from a tree at the edge of the Wolffs' pasture.

All my life I have believed that frost was absolutely essential to the ripening of the wild persimmon. Not so. This year the tree in the woods back beyond the garden was plummeting soft, sweetly flavored persimmons to the ground weeks before we had that first silvering of frost. Mr. Gibbons says time, sunlight and warmth are what it takes to bring the persimmon to perfection.

With wintertime just over the hill, just around the next bend, summer makes a last stand in the country. The sun sets like an old-time vaudevillian making a farewell performance. It seems to need to tell us that it isn't as strong or as bright as it was a while back but it still has the power to streak the west with rose, vermillion and violet and make you stand a while in the gathering dusk and watch it.

The turnips in the garden are tender and crisp and I cropped a basketful, glad the recent rains have made the job of washing them easier and wishing it were possible to cook turnip greens without hot buttery cornbread to go with them.

Now if I had only brought back some persimmon leaves along with the two squashed persimmons in my pocket I might try Euell Gibbons' recipe for tea. It is very high in vitamin C, he says, and maybe so much vitamin C would do something to diminish the fattening effects of turnip greens, pot likker and cornbread.

Christmas

There are a lot of things you can — or must — do with your time in early December but I cast my vote for planting a holly tree. According to ancient lore you dare not put holly in the house until Christmas Eve. Despite the old belief that the name "holly" was derived from "holy" and that the thorny leaves were used to make the crown Jesus wore to His crucifixion, there's an older superstition that says it's bad luck to bring holly into the house until Christmas Eve. It will just set off quarreling and dissention in the household — and who wants that at this loveliest of seasons?

But you can certainly plant one in the yard and I've been planning to buy a tree. Word got around and two neighbors called up and said, "BUY a holly tree? Don't be silly!"

It seems that if you've ever had a fine red-berried American holly tree you're never short on hollies again. They come up all over the place, unbidden and untended.

Ruby Chadwick once had a magnificent parent tree, now gone, but it left behind descendants all over a steep bank near her house. She and her little grandson, Neal, and I spent the noon hour on Saturday balanced precariously on the bank wielding a mattock and a shovel. From this effort I reaped a harvest of three or four little trees.

Then over at Mr. and Mrs. Shawdie Stewart's house there's one of the prettiest holly trees I ever saw. It towers above the roof, white trunk gleaming, its thorny leaves bright with blood-red clusters of berries.

"Thought we never would get a holly tree to live there," Mrs. Stewart said. "I planted one or two and they died and Shawdie tried his hand at it, too. Every time we went fishing it looked like we'd bring home another holly tree and set it out. Finally that one took a-hold."

"When do you think mine will be that big?" I asked.

"Not long," said Mr. Stewart judiciously. "We've only had that one thirty years."

From his vantage point of eighty-three years, Mr. Stewart can easily regard a thirty-year-old tree as a mere stripling but I don't want to wait that long so when the Stewarts gave me my choice of young trees down in the woods past their collard patch I chose the biggest — a six-footer which has already attained the distinctive triangular holly shape. We all dug and chopped at entangling pine roots and tugged and pulled. Mrs. Stewart and I got down on our bellies and rolled under the barbed wire fence but we gently hefted the holly and set it on the other side.

Back at Sweet Apple I hauled woods' dirt and we hacked out a hole in the clay and made a little nest of dark loam, spreading the roots and watering them in. Pushing the wheelbarrow and manning the mattock are hard on the hands but I kept thinking of all the lore about holly. Its healing properties seem endless, if chancy. Indians made a ceremony of drinking tea brewed from yaupon (a member of the holly family), but if a woman moved or walked about during the cooling or serving of the tea the men would pour out the drink, disgorge what they had swallowed and severely punish the transgressing female. The drink was reserved for those who proved to be brave and courageous warriors.

All my trees may die but they're green so far and I go out and look at them every day and feel very fortunate. As long as they live I am protected from witches and thunder and lightning.

FOLLOWING THE EXAMPLE OF THE ATLANTA BIRD CLUB, which decorates a Christmas tree for the birds in Piedmont Park one day each year around the middle of December, I am assembling grapefruit and orange rinds for baskets, cheap peanut butter and clearing last year's dried and weevily raisins out of the cupboard for a similar tree at Sweet Apple.

Maybelle Dickey Hodgins makes a concoction she calls "Margie's Porridge," which all birds love. She uses two parts of ground suet, two parts cornmeal, two parts sugar, one part flour; mixes the ingredients together, adds water (not over one-half part) and cooks, stirring until it thickens. Then she pours it into a well-greased pan to harden. Squares of this, cut like fudge, vanish as speedily on the bird feeder as candy does at a children's party.

A STUDENT WROTE ME A LETTER from the University of Alabama asking for some assurance that the Christmas "feeling" comes every year. Her boy friend is in Vietnam and she doesn't know if it's going to be possible "to feel Christmasy at all."

"But I want to so much," she wrote. "When do you begin to feel it?"

Different times for different people, I had to write her. Many times in life that warm rush of gladness and excitement over Christmas seems late in coming and then it hits you suddenly at an unexpected time and place. Once for me it was on a bus when I tried to struggle home with two little red rockers I hadn't thought I was going to be able to buy. Often it comes when we unpack the Christmas-tree ornaments and take out battered and well-loved things.

This year in the midst of many projects and problems I thought I might have to totter through the season without that sustaining wave of pre-Christmas excitement and delight. Get through it somehow, I thought resignedly, do what is necessary, be as happy as possible and don't count on choking up with joy unconfined.

Then there was the afternoon I was assigned to pick up Bird and Tib at the nursery where they go after school every day to wait for their mama or their daddy to get them. Traffic was heavy and that day I had the pickup truck, which is harder to maneuver through traffic. I felt rushed and tired and distracted. The children came out looking rosy-cheeked and sparkly-eyed from play and clutching a cooky in each hand. They climbed into the truck with pleasure. (It is their favorite vehicle.) And then they saw a Christmas-wrapped box I had on the seat beside me.

"Who's it for?" they wanted to know and I explained that it was a gift to all of us from Mrs. Nelson Severinghaus, a longtime friend. They wanted to open it and with my mind on traffic and the glaring headlights, which were beginning to come on, I distractedly gave them permission.

"Oooooh!" I heard Tib say, with a soft inrush of breath and then Bird whooped.

"Nestes!" he cried. "Nestes for the Christmas tree!"
There was one for each of us — little excelsior nests sprayed
gold with a clothespin attached to hold it to the Christmas
tree and a bright plumaged bird with three tiny glass
ornament eggs on each nest. A note on each said:

> _Especially blessed_
> _And happy is he,_
> _Who finds a bird's nest_
> _In his Christmas tree._
> — Old Swedish Proverb

It took a mile or two for them to pick out the bird
they wanted. They lingered over the decision and finally
settled on a pink bird for Tib and a yellow bird for Bird.

And then they started singing — not together, of
course, but two different songs. It was "Silent Night"
from Bird and "O Tannenbaum!" from Tib. I shut them
up and started them over and we all sang together,
"Silent night, holy night, all is calm, all is bright..."

Suddenly it _was_ calm and bright. The darkness had a
velvety look. Traffic lights twinkled like stars. The voices
of the children rose sweetly — off key and out of tune but
lovely. Christmas, I thought, ah Christmas...it's here.

Everybody has a favorite fantasy, I guess, and the one
that takes a grip on me at this season of the year, driving
me to fresh fits of fruitless activity, is the one my children call "Mama's Gilded Walnut Dream."

This is the season of the year when I think I'm
going to perform marvelous feats toward getting ready for
Christmas by picking up acorns and — yes, walnuts, too —
gilding stuff and sewing and painting and baking and

going the last mile with the loving-hands-at-home routine.

I'M ALWAYS GOING TO ASTOUND MY FAMILY AND FRIENDS by having the most artistic, homemade type Christmas the world has ever seen. I scavenge the woods for perfect pine cones and polished acorns and the elegant fretwork of sweetgum burrs. I spread them out on the terrace and gloat over them like they were freshly dug diamonds. But comes the time to turn them into a sort of tawny gold and Della Robbia wreath for the back door (this is my recurring dream) and I'm lost. There's a need for something I can't find — pliers or chicken wire or glue or maybe just time and talent.

By now I should know it's going to be a pine Christmas. It always has been — swags of pine and cedar over the mantel and along the bannisters, branches tied to the front door with red bows, stuffed in the well bucket, which is also tied with a red bow, and poked into that old tin mold for the kitchen table. (This is a handy centerpiece, if too easy to count. The center of the mold accommodates a fat red candle, the outer part, water to keep sprigs of pine fresh for days.)

For the Christmas Eve supper table I will have the same apple tree I have had since we moved to Sweet Apple. My son gave me a handsome footed glass bowl one year and it is perfect for a pyramid of polished red apples, held together by toothpicks and accompanied by sprigs of boxwood tucked here and there between the apples.

The children help me make it and we eat the apples

that aren't pretty enough for our centerpiece. They are always insistent on seeing the "star" in the center of the apple and hearing for the thousandth time the story which, I found out after I had been telling it for years, a Georgia schoolteacher named Madge Bigham wrote nearly fifty years ago. The small apple tree, so the tale goes, was a good happy-dispositioned little tree with one all-encompassing ambition. After looking at the stars every night she decided that she wanted one for her very own. The fairy queen heard her wish and told her to strive and work to grow strong and beautiful and her wish would be granted. The apple tree did her best and finally one spring day she was covered with beautiful pink blossoms which dropped away, leaving little brown baby seeds that would someday grow into apples.

She was so happy, loving and caring for her baby seeds that she forgot all about her wish but the orchard fairy had not forgotten. The orchard fairy told the apple tree she had earned her wish and she would make her a crown of stars. To do her credit, the tree decided wanting a star for herself was foolish and selfish.

"But if stars you have to give," she reputedly told the fairy, "give them, I pray you, to my baby seeds."

So that is why, if you cut your apple through the center of the circle side, you find brown baby seeds nestled in a five-pointed star.

ONCE OR TWICE IN A LIFETIME you encounter the absolutely perfect present for a person you love. Until John and I went to town to do his Christmas shopping the other day he and Ted had settled on a $1.69 football for their dad's major present.

They bought it days ago, tenderly wrapped it in the complete Sunday edition of the newspaper, affixed Christmas seals and ribbons to it and stowed it where they could take it out and shake it and peek at it occasionally.

But then John and I had the ceremonial day in the stores I try to spend with each of the grandchildren — lunch and a lot of looking. He found a good many twenty-nine-cent kitchen gadgets that his mother needed and a fifty-two-cent fishing lure for his father. We would have been finished with our big safari into the marts of trade if he hadn't found an amazing "safety signal" light designed to be affixed to the roof of an automobile in trouble and plugged into the cigarette lighter.

"I see what I want for my dad," he told me eagerly, tugging at my hand.

I reminded him of the splendid football and the fifty-two-cent lure but he kept going back and looking at the plastic revolving light and his eyes were shining.

"My dad really needs this," he said. "If he had a wreck or anything he could use it."

The price was a staggering $3.99 and his mother had cautioned me to keep his shopping within the limits understood by a little boy. I started to tell him how expensive the revolving blue gadget was but the light in his eye stopped me.

When you find that gift, the absolutely perfect gift for somebody you love, it is a hang-the-expense thing, as urgently important as the gift of the magi. The revolving blue signal light was such a wonder and we got it and I know one young man who is very rich this Christmas.

THE ONLY PEOPLE I KNOW WHO ARE DIFFICULT to shop for are the non-gardeners. With a gardener there is never a problem. Work gloves and flower seeds, clippers and flower-arranging paraphernalia, bird and flower books, pictures and, if you want to go all out (God bless my family), even a load of cottonseed meal or sheep manure.

Plants and trees are great gifts because they are "keepers." The dogwood trees in my front yard were given to me the first Christmas I owned Sweet Apple cabin, the boxwood around the eaves the second Christmas. The sugar maple in the back yard came five years ago — a gift that grows more beautiful with every passing year. I wanted a magnolia tree but I tried not to make a to-do over it because even in the South, in some areas of which wild ones are to be had, they are expensive.

On Christmas Eve family and close friends assemble at Sweet Apple for the Christmas party that precedes the ones they will have in their own homes on Christmas morning. We sang carols, and ate, and exchanged our gifts and I was so busy I didn't notice for a time that one of my gifts seemed to be a piece of string.

When I looked at it in some bewilderment the children dropped their toys and everybody gathered around, crying, "Follow it! Follow it!"

Flashlights were brought and young and old trooped after me as I followed the string out the door, across the terrace and down the hill. There, settled in just where I had dreamed it, was a fifteen-foot magnolia, its polished leaves catching the light from our torches and rustling coldly in the December wind.

"Best of all," said Muv practically, "the hole for it is part of the gift."

But I'm not sure that the hole, magnificent gift that it is in this hard-clay season, is the best part. Nor do I think it is June's bounty of creamy-white deeply fragrant flowers. I think it is the fact that a tree, a green growing tree, is a year-round gift of beauty, a living reminder long after Christmas of imaginative love and caring and generosity.

Epilogue

Since I wrote this book 17 years ago I have edged forward a bit and I have blackslid a bit. My gardening knowledge and accomplishments have been — to use both a scriptural and horticultural reference — no bigger than a mustard seed, but my pleasure in working the earth has doubled and redoubled.

Change hit Sweet Apple settlement almost before the original publication of this book reached the publisher's warehouse. Nearly all my country neighbors have died or sold their land for subdivisions and moved away. These were people who depended on the land for a living and had bred-in-the-bone knowledge and expertise. I grieved for every one of them, particularly those who lived closest.

Almost any spring day one or another could be seen walking down the road, bringing a slip of some plant, a rooted cutting, a shaking of garden seeds. Their kind offerings of sacks full of "leather britches" or dried apples from their own winter supply of vegetables reminded me when planting season came that I should make provision for food to sustain us through the winter. Where, oh, where would you find a nice poke of leather britches these days? Those dried beans strung like jewels on a clean string. They are picked when young and tender — at summer's peak, then hung in an attic or a loft room to dry. This vegetable, cooked with ham or streakedy bacon and seasoned lightly with red pepper, saw many a country family through the cold months when fresh vegetables were nonexistent and canned and frozen ones had not been thought of yet.

Those neighbors were reared in the pioneer custom of sharing. Garden centers and nurseries had still not moved to the boondocks. If they had appeared Sweet Apple citizens were too busy or too financially strapped to seek them out. People didn't BUY plants, particularly ornamental ones then. Vegetable seed, yes — and fertilizer, but flowers were meant to be shared, passed from neighbor to neighbor, handed down from grandmothers and old aunts. It was part of their poetry, their magic.

"That stand of hollyhocks by the barnyard fence, Granny Duncan started that when she was a bride. Would you like some seed?"

"That Dusty Miller, Aunt Lucy brought it over the mountains in a kivvered wagon. It multiplies. Help yourself."

"Mrs. Cox's 'johnny quills' have been there for seventy-five years or more, the earliest and most fragrant in the settlement. Take this trowel and dig yourself an apronful."

Garden bounty obtained from a sharing neighbor was admittedly leisurely about reaching maturity. A slip of boxwood might not look like much for 10 or 15 years. Even the hollyhocks, being biennials, took two years to show themselves. But farm-reared country people were patient. The slow rhythms of the earth and the seasons had conditioned them to plant and tend and wait.

Newcomers to Sweet Apple woods are children of the instant-everything age. Before the houses are finished and long before the owners move into their new homes, landscapers arrive with truckloads of fully grown shrubs and trees, and even flats of blooming annuals.

I have seen — and admired — an instantaneous wild flower garden. Equipped with ready-to-sow collections, city owners had a glorious stand of lupines and daisies, blackeyed Susans and butterfly bush, heal-all and skyblue chicory overnight. Nature, dependent upon wind and birds to scatter seeds, might have pulled it off in half a century.

Creating even a remote resemblance to a lawn around Sweet Apple cabin was an undertaking fraught with failure, uncertainty and chickweed. Our new neighbors, housed in dwellings that cost as much as a million dollars, have no such problems. Before the movers arrived with furniture, lawn crews were on the site covering all reaches of the lots with turf — velvety, emerald, innocent of weeds. They roll it out like carpet and it seems to behave like carpet with its smooth close pile.

CHANGE ALSO CAME to Sweet Apple's "biggin," as the Scots probably would call my homeplace. Every gardener needs a partner, not only to divide the labor of digging, lifting and hauling, but also to share the pleasure of accomplishment. In the cool of the evening when the sweat begins to dry on your brow and you have a moment to sit under a tree and admire your handiwork, the sweet rewards of planting and harvesting need to be shared. I married my gardening companion.

Jack Strong introduced me to Sweet Apple when he bought 20 acres along a little creek half a mile away. I went with him to look at land one Saturday afternoon and saw Sweet Apple's dejected, lopsided little log cabin at the same time. Jack knew nothing about gardening except how to avoid mowing his mother's lawn in Biloxi, Mississippi—an experience of his youth. He once confessed to me that the only trees he could reliably identify were pines and oaks.

It was a different story when he acquired land. He cleared a spot on the creek bank for his first garden. My children and I were enthusiastic participants—it was our first garden, too.

Country-reared, I had some familiarity with woodland plants, and Jack became a diligent student. He liked nothing better than to stroll through his woods learning the names and the growing habits of everything that bloomed or leafed. He transplanted rhododendrons and wild azaleas to the spot where he had a tractor shed with temporary living quarters attached. He brought in young crabapple trees from his aunt's yard in Mississippi and planted them to shelter his well house. He was the fervent admirer and protector of the fragrant sweet shrub by his roadside and the sourwood with its panicles of white blooms so seductive to honey bees.

When I acquired Sweet Apple cabin, Jack transferred his attention and his zeal to its tangled acres. It was his tractor, newly acquired, which cleared the patch of a jungle-like growth of wild plumb and sumac interwoven with honeysuckle and poison ivy. It was he who braved the bottom of the old well, sending up buckets of sludge, one of which contained a small snake. He voted to transfer our vegetable gardening efforts from his creekside patch, which was too shady anyway, to the sunny area back of the cabin, and he plunged headlong into organic lore with all the various methods of composting. He learned early on that I preferred stable manure to diamonds. When my birthday rolled around in May, I could almost count on driving into the backyard and finding a dark, rich-smelling mound with a big sign on it reading, "Happy Birthday, Tine!"

When I expressed an interest in a greenhouse he took me to the University of Georgia's agriculture college in Athens to see how they had executed the plans for a simple inexpensive structure for the home gardener, employing plastic plumbing pipes and sheets of polyurethane. He came home and promptly built one for me.

That greenhouse was eminently successful for a few seasons. I had the huskiest tomato plants at setting-out time that anybody ever saw. All the charming flowers that garden centers were not then stocking flourished under my plastic roof. But it was a good distance from the cabin, being no architectural gem, and I slept undisturbed the night the oil burner — its source of heat — went berserk and covered every inch of my greenhouse's gleaming roof and every plant beneath it, with greasy soot.

A smaller greenhouse, closer to home, one I could keep my eye on while I prepared dinner, one easy to visit between pot stirrings, seemed a desirable successor. Jack persuaded two of my grandsons to help him clear out the little lean-to woodshed adjoining the toolhouse. They spent a day hauling off soggy fireplace logs and years of accumulation of stored debris.

Jack spent a week building a frame to hold sheets of glass he obtained from an ad in our state *Farmers & Consumers Market Bulletin.* He installed a used sink and ran a water hose from the garden. Lights and a small propane gas heater came next, and shelves for seed flats and hooks for hanging baskets followed.

Jack and I were married shortly after this project was finished and we spent many pleasant hours on kitchen stools in the small greenhouse, filling flats with potting soil, pricking off seedlings, watering and planning.

He sometimes thought of expanding it but by that time our woods were filling with new subdivisions and our quiet little country road became noisy with traffic — lumber trucks and concrete mixers, followed by station wagons and imported cars, school buses, mail carriers.

The need to screen out the traffic and the street lights across the road, to retain some semblance of a tranquil green-enclosed old country place, presented a new challenge to Jack. Thereafter, every trip we took included a visit to the area's nursery where we searched for trees and shrubs to plant as a wall of privacy to separate us from the road.

The summer that Jack was stricken with cancer was one of the hottest and dryest in Georgia history. Our backyard was filled with cans of magnolias, hollies and swamp myrtles that didn't seem plantable between the weather and Jack's gradual weakening illness. He never stopped thinking about the greenery he couldn't dig holes for, however, and almost every day found him watering his trees and shrubs, or moving them to bigger pots.

Jack died in November of 1988. The first few weeks afterward, I wondered if I could bear to live longer in the country. The daily trip to the office with the increasing traffic was a battle, and without Jack's help the land of home seemed scraggly and neglected—impossible for a woman alone to tend.

Fortunately, I am not a woman alone. My grandsons, the ones we had hauled around the yard in a wagon hitched to the lawnmower, the ones for whom we bought a billy goat and donkeys, the ones who had learned to swim in Jack's lake, arrived to plant his trees and shrubs.

It took them all of a December afternoon with me hauling water and delivering directions. Then we stood and looked at the little forest of young plants. It will be years before they make an adequate screen against the road, but I knew then that I had to stand by and wait it out. If the time those young plants need to mature is left to me, I'll be spending it at Sweet Apple.

References

Carson, Rachel. *Silent Spring*. 25th anniversary edition. Houghton Mifflin, 1987. P. 68.

Gillespie, Janet. *Peacock Manure and Marigolds*. Viking, 1964. P. 23.

Hadfield, Miles and John Hadfield. *Gardens of Delight*. Little, Brown, 1964. P. 43.

Jefferson, Thomas, *The Garden and Farm Books of Thomas Jefferson*. Ed. Robert C. Baron. Fulcrum, 1988. P. 87.

Parker, Dorothy. *Enough Rope*. Boni & Liveright, 1926. P. 32.

Sackville-West, Vita. *A Joy of Gardening*. Atheneum, 1983. P. 54.

Stopka, Arthur, ed. *Wildflowers in Color*. Harper & Row, 1982. P. 126.

Stouts, Ruth. *How To Have a Green Thumb Without an Aching Back*. Cornerstone Library, 1955. P. 38.

Swain, Ralph B. *The Insect Guide: Orders and Major Families of North American Insects*. Doubleday, 1948. P. 102.

West, Jessamyn. *The Friendly Persuasion*. Harcourt, Brace, 1956. P. 190.

EDITOR'S NOTE: Books mentioned in the text that do not appear in this listing are out of print.